T0193841

Look into Me

Look into Me

BRENDA K. O'BELLA

LOOK INTO ME

iUniverse books may be ordered through booksellers or by contacting:

iUniverse
1663 Liberty Drive
Bloomington, IN 47403
www.iuniverse.com
1-800-Authors (1-800-288-4677)

Because of the dynamic nature of the Internet, any web addresses or links contained in this book may have changed since publication and may no longer be valid. The views expressed in this work are solely those of the author and do not necessarily reflect the views of the publisher, and the publisher hereby disclaims any responsibility for them.

Any people depicted in stock imagery provided by Thinkstock are models, and such images are being used for illustrative purposes only. Certain stock imagery © Thinkstock.

ISBN: 978-1-4917-5174-9 (sc)
ISBN: 978-1-4917-5173-2 (e)

Library of Congress Control Number: 2015902076

Print information available on the last page.

iUniverse rev. date: 5/8/2015

Learning to change the way you see your story is the hardest part of unlocking your truest self.

Chapter 1

*T*HIS IS MY STORY. I WAS BORN AND RAISED IN A SMALL TOWN WITH my mother, Ann, and father, Eddie, along with my three siblings, Tara, David, and Eddie.

At age five, I went to school to paint a picture for my teacher. I told myself I would never get involved with a man who drinks. I voiced this as a little girl because of my parents' constant yelling and fighting. I believed if my dad would just stop drinking, I could have a much better life, just like all the other kids at school. My siblings and I saw food thrown onto our walls. My dad constantly ripped the phone cord out of the wall. I felt afraid to bring friends home. I couldn't predict what my friends would walk into, and I was embarrassed of what they'd say about my environment.

My life moved on. My parents' arguing occurred daily and late at night. One day, my parents were fighting, and my siblings told me to go downstairs and make them stop. They basically threw me down the stairs. At age six, feeling like the strong one, I went downstairs to stop my father and protect my mother from him.

In the middle of the heat of their arguing, my father turned to me with hate in his eyes and yelled, "You're nothing but a special-ed retard! Go back upstairs!"

In return, I screamed, "You're nothing but a drunken, no-good bastard. I hate you! I hate you!" My voice was loud enough that all my siblings could hear me. I ran like hell up the steps, as fast as I could. I felt so proud to be the one to stand up to him. The words and label he gave me were true; I was in special-education classes. I did not have the ability to comprehend what I was reading, which affected everything I had to attempt to learn.

As time passed, with every ounce of me, I tried to do better in school. I gradually noticed a difference in myself and started to get better grades. During this time, I never talked to or even looked at my father. If anything, it was a one-word question or answer. I avoided any kind of father-daughter connection. In a really short period of time, I did well enough to get out of the special class I was in. I worked until I reached all regular classes, and I was so proud to be there.

Years passed. I did better in school. I didn't allow myself to talk to my father because of what he said to me. He didn't deserve me. I believed I was so much better than he was. I was no longer in special classes. *He'll never change,* I thought. *He's still an alcoholic and a no-good bastard.*

I believed these thoughts, and I became stronger in my beliefs about what is wrong and right. I also felt as if I was perfect because of what I had accomplished in school. I graduated as an honor student in all regular classes. I believed I was going in the right direction.

I finished high school and headed into the normal, real world. I started dating a kid named Joe, who forced himself to date me. I didn't believe he was my type or feel any kind of physical connection with him. For the most part, all I really did was push him away. Any words that Joe said to me, I often thought or felt them to be negative and against me.

I dated Joe for eight years. I always felt as if something was missing within him, but I was unable to put my finger on it. He's a really hardworking guy. I knew he loved me in ways that really didn't matter to me. He seemed very protective of me and jealous of other kids who liked me. Joe took over his father's roofing and siding company, which his father had established many years before he passed away.

We got married on November 29, 1997, a picture-perfect day. The weather was so beautiful. I felt so nervous. I felt fake for allowing my father to walk me down the aisle. It felt wrong, but it also seemed like the right thing to do and what my mother wanted me to do.

I did not have any kind of emotional connection with my dad. At the reception, my dad and I danced to the song "Daddy's Little Girl." I didn't want to dance with him. But again, I felt it was the right thing for me to do. I didn't say much to him during our dance.

During our dance, my dad voiced to me, "You're a really good kid!" I smirked. He said, "You never gave me any trouble. You always did the right thing. I'm proud of you, Brenda!"

I could feel myself getting choked up. I could not believe he had waited all this time to voice all that to me, not to mention on my wedding day in the middle of our dance with two hundred people staring at us. I only wanted him to shut up and stop talking. I kept nodding to him, but I would not say anything. My thought: *Let's get this dance over with.*

I knew my mom probably told him to say all that bullshit. After our dance, I couldn't wait to get away from him. He was saying all these nice things to me, but I didn't know how to handle it.

Our reception was nice, with all our family and friends there with us. Joe struggled with the fact that his father was not with us. For our honeymoon, we went to Mexico. We enjoyed our time together.

Chapter 2

*J*OE AND I PURCHASED A FIXER-UPPER HOME ABOUT TEN MINUTES away from our parents. Because Joe did roofing and siding, he did most of the work himself. When we first moved in, we did not have much. There were no kitchen or walls in our house. We lived in our bedroom, which contained the only furniture we had. Little by little, we got more and more things as we could afford them.

Time passed. Our house became our home. Our grass was always cut and looked really nice, picture-perfect from the outside looking in. For years together, we lived up to the perfectness of that appearance.

Joe and I decided to have a baby. My pregnancy was complicated by gallbladder issues, which kept me in pain for the duration of the pregnancy. My doctor was not able to do surgery until I delivered the baby. Living in the amount of pain I had, I felt that if I hadn't gotten pregnant, I would not have been in this pain because the doctors could do the surgery right away. I felt a lot of bitterness toward my unborn child and Joe.

My sister, Tara, said, "Just wait until you hear the baby's heartbeat." I heard the baby's heartbeat but felt nothing.

My mom said, "Once you feel life, you will love this baby." The baby kicked, but I felt no connection. I only wanted to get this baby out and have the surgery. Once my son Joseph was born on November 13,

1998, I had the surgery. Then the gallstones were gone, relieving the tremendous physical pain I was in.

I struggled to find any kind of connection with Joseph because of all the pain I still felt. I couldn't let anyone know what I was actually feeling. I thought to myself, *I'm not normal. This is not normal. I'm supposed to love this baby. I should want to hold him and talk baby talk with him. What's wrong with me?*

I was scared to death, but I didn't want anyone to think I couldn't do it. I didn't want anyone to know I couldn't handle him. I didn't hold him much the first couple of weeks. I did the daily necessary things for him: feed, bathe, change, and dress. Most of the time, I sat next to him and watched him scream. I didn't want to pick him up.

A few months later, Joseph was playing in his bouncy seat while I was doing housework. I walked past him, and I saw his head facing down. It looked as if his head was hanging over the side of the bouncy seat. I thought he had died.

I screamed, "Oh my God! Oh my God, please! Please let him be okay!"

As I picked Joseph up, he awoke from a sound sleep. I automatically started kissing him, talking to him, and holding him the way I should have when he was born.

"Thank you, God!"

From that day on, I discovered that I loved him more than life itself.

Chapter 3

$\mathcal{L}$IFE WAS MOVING. EVERYTHING WAS GOING WELL. A FEW YEARS passed. Joe and I decided to have another child. This pregnancy was emotionally bad. Twenty weeks into the pregnancy, I got prenatal testing for spina bifida and Down syndrome. The results came back positive for spina bifida.

My gynecologist went over my options. One was to terminate the pregnancy. They didn't encourage me to do it, but they needed me to know and understand the needs and complications of having a baby and then adult living with spina bifida. I chose to have the baby and accept whatever God was willing to give me. For the duration of the pregnancy, I went twice a week for a stress test.

On October 18, 2002, I delivered a beautiful little girl. We named her Gracie Rose. She was the most beautiful little girl I'd ever seen. She did not have spina bifida. She was 100 percent normal—just perfect.

A couple of weeks passed. I took Gracie for a routine blood exam. The results from the test said that Gracie had a blood disease called glucose-6-phosphate dehydrogenase. I was scared to death. I told the doctor all about the pregnancy, regarding the spina bifida they thought she had. The doctor said that Gracie's condition was not related in any way. The doctor suggested taking Gracie to a children's hospital in the city, which wasn't what I wanted to hear.

A few days later, I was driving in my hometown on a road I usually do not travel on. As I was driving, I passed my childhood church, where I had made all my sacraments and gotten married. I glanced over and saw "God bless Gianna" on a sign out in front of the church. This sign looked neon to me.

My mother called as I was passing this church. She said, "How about you bring Gracie over to Mass today? I heard they are having Saint Gianna Beretta Molla. She has been known to bless mothers and babies, and they may be able to bless Gracie!"

I said, "Oh my God, you're not going to believe this, Mom; I am driving past it now. I just saw the sign 'God bless Gianna.'"

My mom said, "Really? Go back over there. I'll meet you at the church."

I said, "Mom, I must go in and see what this is all about." I felt as though I was meant to be there.

As we walked in, a woman walked over to me and said, "We're having a Mass for Gianna Beretta Molla. She is trying to be canonized as a saint."

They walked us up to the altar with Gianna Molla's gloves, hat, and dress, along with some holy water. The woman placed all of Gianna Beretta Molla's belongings on my daughter and blessed her with the holy water. We stayed for the Mass. At the time, I did not truly believe in the Catholic religion or that saints had any ability to help me. The experience amazed me.

A few days went by; we had Gracie's blood retested, and the results were 100 percent normal. Gracie had no signs of having anything wrong with her.

At the time, because of my beliefs and thoughts, I was too ashamed to say what I felt. This must have been a miracle; however, I did not want to tell others. It was kind of like wanting to believe in the miracle of it and knowing others could never understand.

More information on Gianna Beretta Molla can be found at http://saintgianna.org, which says she was a wife, mother, doctor, and prolife witness, and she was canonized in Rome on May 16, 2004.

It took me a few months to send in my testimony:

"God gave her a sign—an actual sign!"

Chapter 4

A FEW MORE YEARS PASSED. JOE AND I LOOKED LIKE AND THOUGHT of ourselves as the perfect couple. Our son, Joseph, was about six years old and our daughter, Gracie, age three. Joe started acting out in rage; he was extremely angry. The look in his eyes scared me. The words he said to me were extremely hurtful.

He would scream, "You don't love me! I can't feel love from you. I feel like killing someone." But then he would make me a nice dinner and always have a plate on the table for me. He always helped out with cleaning the house and bathing the kids, all after he had worked on a roof.

His verbal abuse was really hard for me to deal with. I felt really alone and afraid to tell anyone. They could never imagine Joe would ever be so verbally abusive to only me. Because of the tone in his voice and the words he said, I felt rage and anger, so I often yelled back at him.

Also, our sex life during this time was not the same. I did not feel any real connection. When we had sex, it was rough, an act of body-to-body motions—more like actions instead of making love or having a connection. He was distant yet connected in other ways. He always told me to eat.

I often told myself, *I will never allow my kids to grow up around all this angriness, like I did as a child. I am not going to live in the mess, like my mother. She put up with a lot of bullshit for years from my father. I am going to take my kids and move somewhere. Anywhere is better than living with this monster.*

I didn't want to live in the same town, let alone house, with Joe. I believed I was at the lowest point in my life. I built up enough courage to reach out and tell my mother. I told her everything Joe was creating. I blamed him for everything that was happening and all that was wrong. I could not understand why Joe was so extremely angry. It came out of nowhere.

My mother was in complete disbelief of his words. I tried to describe the look in his eyes to her; he looked as though he wasn't even in there. He was completely crazy and an out-of-control monster! But I knew a part of my heart wanted someone to help him. Some days, he cried hysterically, and then he'd say how sorry he was; he did not mean what he was saying.

With a monsterlike stare in his eyes, he screamed to me, "I just want to kill myself, Brenda! Is that what you want me to do? If you tell me to, I'll do it!" He also voiced, "I just want to kill someone with my bare hands." I was so overwhelmed and confused.

Every Sunday, Joe and I went to his mother's house for Sunday spaghetti dinner. All of Joe's family met there. I asked his mom, Annette, to help him. I told her, "I'm leaving Joe." I said, "Look, Annette, you do not understand! Your son is acting like he could really kill someone. You need to help him."

She asked, "What do you want me to do?"

I looked at her with such a disgusted look. "I don't know—nor do I care. Just do something. Talk to him. Tell him that you love him! Hug him! I really don't give a shit what you do. Just do something."

I was pissed. I felt as if she didn't even care about him. She had no emotions, like it was a calm day. She started complaining about the butter that was on the table. I lost it.

I asked, "Are you kidding me? Your son is acting like a completely crazy maniac! All you want to talk about is the butter on the table—that it doesn't taste right? Really?"

I didn't have the best relationship with Annette at that time. She has a hard time expressing what she's feeling. When Joe and I got married

I could keep it in, but the rage in his eyes looked like the devil. As I reached out to my mom and explained it to her, she seemed to always justify Joe's behavior. She seemed to understand Joe more than she did me. At the time, I felt as if I didn't matter much to her.

My mom was an amazing woman and was loved by so many. Many friends and family members went to her with their problems. She always knew the right words to say to ease everyone around her. But I felt anger toward her. I was her daughter. I wished she could look into me; maybe then she'd understand me—maybe tell me how right I was.

Joe felt really comfortable talking to my mom. Joe went over to her house for visits. They got into deep conversations. He told her secrets about being molested by a man when he was just a young boy.

One day, I was ready and wanting to leave Joe. We had argued badly that morning. I called my mom to tell her what Joe had said to me. My mom asked me to come over to her house. I didn't know Joe was already there. She sat me down next to Joe.

My mother asked Joe, "Do you love Brenda?"

He answered, "Yes, I do."

My mom sat right in front of us. She placed one of her hands on his knee and her other hand on mine. She looked at me and asked, "Do you love Joe?"

I said, "Yeah, but he looks like the devil, Mom!"

She asked, "Brenda, do you love him?"

I said, "Yeah," and I started to cry.

She asked us to repeat the words "I love you" several times to each other. I was still fearful of him and really didn't want to tell him that I loved him. His face was extremely red. He looked like he was about to burst. We stayed there for a little while, and things between us were okay and mendable for the moment.

Joe knew for years that my mother's father had molested her. She openly talked about the abuse to me and my siblings when we were children and got into more details as we got older. When I was a little girl, my mom said to me, "Don't you ever go over to Pop's house alone." Pop lived in walking distance from our house.

I said, "Why?"

Mom said, "Because I don't trust him!"

I said, "Why?"

My mom said, "He did some things to me that were not appropriate!" I believe that was the start of my mom's communication with me about her father.

My mom understood Joe in a way I couldn't. Therefore, she tried to get me to understand what he had gone through as a child. I just could not understand how his childhood had anything to do with the look in his eyes today.

Chapter 6

A FEW WEEKS LATER, JOE AND I WERE AT OUR WORST. I CALLED HIS sister Elizabeth to come over and talk to him. I also called Annette and asked her if she could watch our kids. Annette could tell from my voice that something was wrong with me.

Annette said, "Sure, I'll watch them. Drop 'em off."

I went over to her house. Annette asked, "Brenda, are you okay?"

I said, "Yeah, I'm okay. I'll be back in a few hours to pick them up."

Annette said, "Sure. No problem. Take your time."

Joseph and Gracie sat there quietly. I kissed them both and left to go home. Without my knowing, Joe had called my mother to come over that same night to talk to me. I was nuts that night. I screamed at Joe, with every curse word I knew, in front of Elizabeth and my mother.

Joe said, "This is just not working."

I yelled, "You're goddamn right this is not working! You need to get out of here! I can't do you another minute."

Joe walked over to where my mother was with his head down. He started to cry and said, "I think I need to go talk to someone."

My mom said, "Joe, that would probably be a good idea."

Elizabeth chimed in. "Joe, do you want me to call someone for you?"

Joe said, "Okay, yeah, make me an appointment."

I screamed at Joe, "I am completely done! I will not speak for you! I will not put another word in your mouth. I will not ask you a question and then allow you to nod your head for you to just agree with whatever I say! That's all done with—and I mean done, done! You're a big boy; it's time you start acting like one. If you're going to continue living in this house, know that I am done with trying to build you up."

The next day, Elizabeth made an appointment for Joe. He went to see the therapist, Dr. Samantha Delomiccon, who specialized in men and women sexually abused as children. He went twice a week to "crisis therapy." Joe called his doctor by her first name.

crying. My cell phone rang. I picked it up. I could not talk. No words would come out. I just kept crying. I hung up the phone.

Five minutes later, my mom called. Then Joe called. Then my mom phoned again. I wanted to talk to them, but I did not have any words to say. Therefore, I decided not to answer their phone calls and turned off my phone. I drove many hours, crying so hard that I could not see. I then pulled into a hospital emergency parking lot so I could just cry. I sat there for ten hours straight. I didn't know a person was capable of crying that hard for that long of a period. It was nothing I had ever experienced before. All my life, I did my best not to cry.

I tried to justify my actions. *At least I didn't bruise her. It's not like I beat her. All I really did was pinch her. She won't hate me. She'll understand,* I told myself over and over in my head. But all along, I was crying, out of control, just trying to understand. I kept seeing the look she had on her face. I believed Gracie hated me—that she'd never talk to me or want to hug me ever again. All my thoughts were completely mixed up and making me feel like a no-good bastard.

Early the next morning, as the sun was coming up, I went home and headed straight into Gracie's room. I woke her up. I was still crying. "I'm so sorry," I said. "Please don't hate me. Please forgive me. I'll never hurt you like that again." I was crying so hard that my stomach was moving in and out uncontrollably.

Gracie tried to console me. She kept saying, "Mommy, it's okay. It's okay." All the while, she was rubbing my head.

Joe came in and lay down on the bed with me. He was also trying to console me. Nothing they said or did seemed to calm me down. I sat on Gracie's bed in a ball, repeatedly saying, "I'm so sorry!"

Joe was twirling my hair and holding me. "Are you okay? What can I do? I love you, Brenda." Joe asked Gracie to go into the other room and watch TV. Joe started to kiss me and rub my back. He tried to help me feel better. Then we had sex.

Now, something about Joe was changing. I noticed he was getting better as an individual. I was feeling mixed, negative emotions between a no-good bastard and my beautiful little girl. I felt I was trying hard to just function. I worked full-time, dealing with the kids and myself.

Joe was still going to see Samantha. He explained to her what I had done to Gracie. He told Samantha how I'd been acting. Samantha explained to him what I was dealing with and suggested a therapist for me. In a way, I knew I needed help, but also, I was embarrassed to go.

After a couple of weeks of me crying off and on, Joe said to me, "Brenda, you need help. Please go talk to the therapist Samantha has suggested. If I can go and do it, I know you can do it too."

Chapter 8

WITHIN THE NEXT FEW DAYS, I MADE MYSELF AN APPOINTMENT with the therapist, Dr. Patel. I waited in fear as my appointment came closer. The day of my appointment, I was a nervous wreck.

Dr. Patel opened the door and asked me to come in. I walked in, still full of nervous emotions. Dr. Patel's first words to me were, "What brings you in to see me? How are you feeling?"

I started crying again. I felt afraid that he would say something that would allow me to break.

He said, "Describe to me what you're feeling."

I said, "I feel fragile, like I'm breakable or porcelain." I was still crying, trying to hold myself together and wondering what he thought of me. My voice was cracking. "I feel like a no-good bastard." But quickly after I said it, I wanted to take back those words. I kept thinking, *He's just going to judge me. He can't help me. He thinks I'm nuts.*

He asked, "Why?"

I explained to Dr. Patel that I had pinched my daughter, Gracie, when she had done nothing to deserve it. I also explained how bad I was feeling. I said, "I am married to a man who is going through a difficult time." I told him that Joe was going to Dr. Samantha Delomiccon. Dr. Patel knew Dr. Delomiccon. His office was right next to hers.

Over the course of many weeks of seeing him, we talked about my childhood and how my parents had reacted toward one another. For the very first time, I said something that I had never talked about with anyone in my life. I explained my dad to Dr. Patel.

I voiced that my dad was a very hard worker. He worked at the steel mill. My mom was a stay-at-home mom. I thought their relationship was terrible. They fought all the time. We didn't have much money. All of us kids stayed up extremely late to protect our mom. We needed to know she was safe. My dad would shove her around sometimes, wanting money to go to the bar. I could remember my dad throwing spaghetti onto the wall on a weekly basis. He ripped the phone cord out of the wall because he didn't want to walk under it when he came home. If my dad was not working or sleeping, he was drinking. I could never understand why my mother stayed with him and why she put up with his bullshit.

I remembered when we got a new washer and dryer. I asked my mom to keep the boxes so we could take them back to the canal to live in. I said, "Mom, please … let's please save these boxes. You can have one all to yourself. Tara, Eddie, David, and I will all fit in the other one."

As I voiced this to Dr. Patel, I started to cry even more. I really believed living at the canal would be better than living with that bastard. He was a monster! I just wished my mom would have left him. I couldn't understand why she hadn't. She put up with a bunch of bullshit way too long. Both Dr. Patel and I smiled, knowing, as an adult, that leaving could possibly lead to even worse living conditions.

I said, "That's how I saw it as a little girl. I always wondered what others lived like. I thought about asking the kids at school if they had to stay up late and watch their parents argue from the top step so their parents didn't see them. But I never did. I felt too ashamed and embarrassed to ask anyone."

I said that my dad was the kind of man who made sure we four kids always had food, clothes, and a roof over our heads. But he never told us he loved us; he wasn't the hands-on kind of dad.

I explained my dad's childhood—at least what I had learned from my mom. He was the third of four children. His mother worked very hard to make ends meet. Her husband, my grandfather, was not in my dad's life. My grandmother had moved away from her husband. He stayed upstate. He was sick and physically abusive toward my grandmother. My dad loved his father. His dad was never abusive to him or the other kids.

My grandmother took her four children and moved four hours away from her husband. She worked in a factory and had to iron clothes to make ends meet. She was a tough, strong, independent woman who was going to make it on her own.

Their neighbor killed Katelyn, my dad's youngest sister, in a drunk-driving incident. Shortly after his sister was killed, my dad went upstate with his aunt and uncle for the summer. My dad played in the woods and mines as a child. When my dad came home, no one explained or talked to him about Katelyn's death. My grandmother never talked negatively about the woman who killed her daughter. The woman never did jail time. They didn't have DUIs back then.

As a young man, my father enlisted in the marines during the Vietnam War. When my dad came back, my parents got an apartment and had their first baby. My father came back from Vietnam a completely different man. I explained all the mixed stories of my life to Dr. Patel, on and on and on.

One day, I was speaking my story to him, and all these lightbulbs were going off in my head. I started to understand more. I could understand why I had pinched Gracie. I felt some kind of relief. For the first time in my life, I needed to forgive my father in the worst way. I had no clue how or when; I just knew in my heart it was time.

Chapter 9

*I*T WAS MY TIME TO LEARN FORGIVENESS. SHORTLY AFTER THE lightbulbs went off in my head, I sat down to write my father a letter explaining everything that I had felt as a young girl because of him. I poured my heart out to him. I felt so much relief and peace. As I was writing the words to my dad, many emotions came to the surface, and it seemed to me that my words became my light. I had never felt so good. I felt like a perfectly imperfect woman. The peace completely amazed me. For the first time in my life, I felt at ease. I understood my father and myself.

I mailed the letter to my parents' house. When my dad read the letter, he thought the letter I poured my heart into was against him. My mom called me on the telephone while she explained to my dad what the letter meant to me. My mother reread the letter to him.

My mom said, "Ed, this letter is not against you! This is Brenda's way of explaining herself. This is a good letter! Brenda has explained to you that she forgives you. Read the bottom sentence, Ed!"

My dad read the last sentence. "I love you, Daddy."

My mom said, "See, Ed? Brenda forgave you! She loves you!"

My dad said, "Look at all the other stuff she said in the letter."

My mom said, "Yeah, Ed! She is saying all that to you because she realizes she is not perfect. She did the same thing to her daughter in a different way."

My dad shook his head. "I don't want to be the bad guy anymore."

My mom said, "You're not the bad guy, Ed. Brenda forgives you! She loves you!"

My dad had a hard time believing the letter was my way of truly forgiving him and healing myself.

Chapter 10

AFTER THIS, MY MARRIAGE BECAME PEACEFUL AND HEALTHY. JOE and I were so connected; he treated me better. He told me often that he loved me. I started to accept all that he was and appreciated all he did for our family. I learned throughout our marriage that Joe always tried to do everything for me to make my life easier. He always did the laundry, gave the kids their baths, and cleaned the house for me. I understood all the hard work Joe did with Samantha to become such a better man. I also realized I didn't feel the need to make myself vomit anymore. Those thoughts were no longer there. I did not need to control anything on the outside.

Both of us felt great as individuals. Our marriage and kids were really, truly happy. One could actually see it in our kids' smiles. Our life moved on in such a positive direction. In my mind, nothing could stop us.

A year passed. One day, my friend Alexa came over to take Gracie and me to lunch. As I was ordering my lunch at the counter, I started to feel light-headed. I asked the young girl at the counter for a Pepsi and said I didn't feel very well. As I said those words, I passed out and fell to the ground. I scared everyone around me. I was on the floor.

My daughter was screaming, "Mommy! Mommy!"

I could hear her voice as I was starting to come to. As I awakened, all these people were around me. The paramedics came in. I was so embarrassed. I saw my shoes were not on my feet.

I said, "Oh my God. I'm okay. I'll be okay."

The paramedic said, "This is not normal for you to pass out like this. You really should come with us to the hospital to get checked out."

With hesitation, I decided to go. Alexa drove to the hospital with Gracie.

After I arrived at the hospital and the paramedics checked my vital signs, I felt fine. I felt that I was wasting everyone's time. The nurse came in and took some blood from me. She asked me many questions, including, "When was your last menstrual cycle?"

I said, "I'm not sure. I do not have a regular menstrual cycle. My periods have always been abnormal."

She asked, "Do you have any children?"

I said, "Yes, I have two."

She said, "Okay."

The nurse left the room with the vials of blood in her hand. As I sat there, I called Joe and explained the story to him. Joe came to the hospital. Meanwhile, Alexa called my mom, who also came to the hospital.

Right before my mom and Joe got there, the nurse walked into the room. She had a huge smile on her face. "Honey, I have great news for you! You're pregnant!" I looked at her in disbelief. She said, "Not only are you pregnant, you're fifteen weeks."

As she was walking around the room, cleaning up and doing her paperwork, I was still puzzled. I was not expecting what she had just said to me to be true. I asked, "Are you joking? Are you sure? Have I been punked? How did this happen?" As I was laughing, I said, "I have two children. I believe I would know, especially if I am fifteen weeks pregnant. I'm not even showing."

She said, "Oh, no, honey, I couldn't joke about something like that."

I smiled in pure joy and disbelief.

When Joe, my mom, Alexa, Joseph, and Gracie came into my room, I told them I was going to have a baby really soon and that I was fifteen weeks pregnant. Everyone was so happy and excited.

The next day, I went to get an ultrasound and saw a baby on the screen. I was so happy and open to having a little baby in our home. Joe and I were amazed we had a baby growing inside my belly and that I had not showed any signs of being pregnant.

At first, the pregnancy went well. However, in the second trimester, I started feeling pain in my right side under my ribs. The pain felt like boiling water dripping under my skin. I dealt with it. I had learned how to deal with physical pain for long periods because of the gallbladder issues with my son, Joseph.

Weeks went by. I started running high fevers. I had extreme sweats and chills in and out of the tub. I felt like complete shit. The pain felt as if boiling water was bursting throughout my belly. Joe drove me to the hospital. I was frantic, thinking that I was in labor. I thought, *Oh my God! I am only eight months. I cannot go into labor now. My baby may be sick.*

I got into the hospital bed. The doctor requested a bunch of tests. Nurses constantly came in to check on me. My fever would not drop. The boiling-water feeling was extreme. They kept me in the hospital for eight days while running tests. Doctors had no idea what the problem was. I kept complaining about the boiling-water sensation in my right side.

Eventually, they gave me antibiotics that brought down my fever and told me that I had two separate issues. One was a kidney infection, and the other—the boiling-water feeling—was a gallbladder duct acting up. Putting both of these together made it complicated for the doctors to diagnose and treat my issues.

For the next two months, I still had the extreme pain of boiling water and walked around with my arm tucked under my rib, trying to stop or help the burning. On November 22, 2008, I delivered another beautiful baby girl. We named her Kathryn. She was awesome. The delivery went well with no complications.

We took Kathryn home. We were so excited to have a baby in the house again. Joseph and Gracie were awesome with their little sister. They helped out and loved her so much. Kathryn was the apple of our eye. The boiling-water feeling under my skin gradually went away.

Two months later, I started feeling the boiling water again. I thought, *I am going to get this checked out. I do not want to ever feel this pain ever, ever again.* In addition, I was thinking about how I had not gotten my period since I had delivered Kathryn and suspected I could be pregnant. Nevertheless, because I did not have a regular period, I didn't think too much about it.

After work a week later, I decided to get a pregnancy test. I went home and took the test. It was positive. I was pregnant.

"Oh my God!" I yelled out with a frantic tone in my voice. "Joe, come here!" He came in, and I said, "Oh my God! I'm pregnant again."

He said, "Hold on. Calm down. Let's talk about this."

I yelled, "Oh no! I cannot. I will not … do this! I just cannot do it. You don't understand. I'm not doing this."

In fifteen minutes, I ran upstairs to get on the Internet, looking for abortion clinics to terminate the pregnancy.

Joe came upstairs with a calm voice and said, "Brenda, I will do whatever it takes … whatever you need me to do! I will do it. I will take care of the baby. You will not need to do anything."

I yelled, "There is absolutely no possible way I'm going through with that pain again. I am not having this baby. I do not care what you say, do, or think! You'll never be able to take this pain away. I am going to terminate this pregnancy. You cannot carry this baby for me, can you?"

Joe replied, "No," and he put his head down, with his hands covering his head.

Joe and I did not talk after I said that. The next day, I called my gynecologist and explained what I planned to do.

He said, "You are not in any shape to be having a baby."

I really did not need his approval. I knew there was no way on earth that I could carry a baby. I felt 120 percent sure of my decision to terminate this pregnancy.

I started talking to one of my old childhood friends and a close family friend; her name is Lacey. I wasn't really close to her at the time, but in some way, I knew she wouldn't judge me or my decision. I also knew she wouldn't tell anyone.

I simply said to Lacey, "Look, I'm pregnant. I made an appointment to terminate this pregnancy next Wednesday."

She said, "Don't you worry, Bren. I got you."

I said, "I need you to pick me up really early that morning. Are you sure you will be able to take me?"

With a much louder tone in her voice, she said, "I got you!"

I said, "Look, you are just a ride for me. Do not ask me any questions. Don't even try to change my mind."

Once again, Lacey yelled, "I effin' got you!"

I smiled back at her.

Wednesday morning came. Lacey and I got into my truck. Lacey noticed a letter on the seat. It was from Joe.

I said, "Don't even think about opening that! Wait until I do what I need to do first. I need to get this done. I cannot hear anything he has to say. He may try to change my mind. Joe wants me to have this baby, but there's no way I can do it. He must not get how much pain I was in."

Lacey said, "Okay, then. You can read it later."

I did not want Joe to take me because I knew he might try to change my mind. I couldn't tell my mother. She'd try too.

Lacey drove me to the clinic. As we approached the parking lot, there stood a priest staring me right in the eye. He was pointing his finger at me, crossing his fingers with pure disgust in his eyes that said, *Shame on you! Shame on you!*

I saw what he was doing and put down my head. Lacey was angry at the priest for doing that to me. She thought he was bothering me. "Bren, don't you worry about him," Lacey said and rolled her eyes.

I said, "Lacey, that man does not bother me one bit. He does not have a clue how I am feeling or my reasons for why I am doing this—not that it matters anyway."

Once I had the procedure, we were starving. We went to get some lunch. I felt so much relief. Then Lacey drove me home. I talked to Joe a little. Then I called my mom and told her.

My mom said, "Brenda, there's no way you could carry a baby! I am glad you made the right decision for you. That would be impossible for you. Why didn't you tell me?"

"I couldn't," I said. "I was too afraid you would try to change my mind."

I did not expect my mom to react that way and be so supportive of me. I 120 percent knew that I had already made the right decision for myself. My mom never frowned on my choice. I only told close family and friends.

Chapter 11

$\mathcal{M}$Y LIFE WENT ON. I HAD THREE BEAUTIFUL KIDS. JOE AND I WERE doing great. We had never been so happy together. We felt a true connection because of all the therapy we both got as individuals. I felt so thankful for having Joe in my life and for his directing me to do the work on myself.

As time passed, about a year later, I gradually started to feel a little distant from Joe. I didn't want to have sex or make love as I used to. Something started happening to me. I started dressing a little sexier. I made sure my hair and makeup were done perfectly for work. It just so happened that people around me were starting to notice I had changed for the better. Many people in my life voiced to me how smart I was, how nice I looked. Men at Wawa flirted with me more and said my legs were sexy. Guys had flirted with me in the past, but I started to enjoy this kind of attention. Therefore, I would smile back at them. I flirted as if I had done it before.

One morning, I got a text message from an unknown number. It said, "Ask your husband about me."

I thought to myself, *What is this?* I asked Joe, "Do you recognize the number?"

He said, "No."

I texted the number back, "Who are you?"

The person texted back, "Don't worry about who I am. Ask your husband. LOL!"

This pissed me off. I texted back, "I'm sorry. I don't know who you are."

There was no response. Now, I was getting really pissed and curious about who this girl was. Later that night, I got another text. It read, "I got cards to prove it."

I texted back, "Well, bring them over so I can see them! Who are you?" and I asked Joe, "What the hell is going on?"

Joe said, "Nothing. I never saw that phone number. I have no idea who that is!"

Early the next morning, my friend Lacey called me, asking, "Where is Joe?"

I said, "He's running to the bank."

She said, "No, he's at this girl's house, flipping out."

All these emotions were running through me. I said, "Lacey, I'm going over there." She gave me the directions to this girl's house. I hung up the phone, grabbed Kathryn, and drove to her house. I walked in to Joe screaming at this girl. The girl looked miserable.

I said to her in a very calm voice, "Do you have something you want to show me?"

She looked at Joe and yelled, "Do I have something to show her, Joe?" She had a cocky tone to her voice.

Joe looked filled with anger. Again, he looked as if he could kill someone.

She yelled again, "Joe, do I have something to show her?" She was also texting someone on her phone.

Joe yelled, "Show her whatever the hell you got! I don't give a shit anymore!" and he walked out the door. As he was walking out, he looked at me and said, "This bitch is crazy."

Again, I asked her, "Do you have something to show me?"

She said, "What are you going to do to me?"

I said to her, "I will not do anything. I just want to see whatever you have."

She went into her bedroom and came out with about ten cards and a few letters from Joe. I started to read them. Nothing made sense to me. My mouth got completely dry.

I asked, "Can I have a drink of water?"

She pointed to the kitchen as she was still texting on her phone. I got up and got myself some tap water.

She said, "A couple years ago, Joe and I had sex."

As I was reading the letters, not able to gather my thoughts, I said, "When?"

She said, "About four years ago. He would stop by here all the time."

I said, "When?"

She said, "We used to meet at five thirty in the morning before work. Joe made me promise him that I would never tell anyone! And I kept my promise. I told Joe that I would never show anyone these cards or tell anyone what we did together."

My thoughts were all messed up. I asked, "Really? Did you love him?"

She said, "Yeah."

"Did he love you?"

She said, "Yeah, but he also told me he loved you. He had sex with me a lot in the beginning. But I wanted affection from him, and he wouldn't give it to me."

I looked at her with a blank stare. I had known this girl for a very brief time in my life. Back then, when Joe and I were doing really badly, she called me a few times, saying negative things about Joe. I could remember her truck being parked at the end of my driveway, closer to my neighbor's house. She called me pretty often. She told me that I deserved better than Joe.

As I was leaving her house, I gave her the glass of water. "Thank you for letting me know. Just woman to woman, do yourself a favor; don't give yourself away to someone who doesn't give you affection. You deserve better than that!"

I truly felt bad for this girl. I left her house in complete shock with all these thoughts running through my mind. I didn't know what to ponder. I thought to myself, *What am I going to do? I just had sex with Joe last night.*

I wanted to leave him then. Why hadn't he just left me? Why had he gone to a therapist to get help? I started to remember everything that Samantha had said and then everything Joe had said. Now I was faced with what this girl had just said. I could remember everything from back then, full blown.

I called my friend Lacey. "I have a letter that Joe wrote to her to show him I have proof."

Lacey said to me, "I will meet you at your house."

I got off the phone with Lacey and drove to Walmart to get cleaning supplies. I purchased two of every cleaning product they had and went home.

I didn't cry or even get angry. I was completely mixed the hell up. In shock, as soon as I got to my house, I started cleaning. I have a clean house anyway, but I cleaned every room, top to bottom.

Lacey picked up my brother David and came over to my house. A little while later, my neighbor came over. She walked in and said, "Damn, girl, what's going on? Damn. I heard about Joe and that girl. She texted me when you guys were there and recorded the conversation. I could hear Joe screaming at her." My neighbor was smiling as she told me her version of the story.

Now, I was really feeling humiliated. "Yes, it's true."

She said, "Yes, I know it's true. That girl sat in her car on our street. Don't you remember?"

I said, "Yeah, I remember."

My neighbor started to tell me how she would talk bad about me to her and ask my neighbor what size jeans I wore. Seeing her truck that day, I could now remember it being parked on our street.

After my neighbor left, I started cleaning, cleaning, and cleaning. Lacey and David were playing with Kathryn in the living room.

My mom came over. She said, "There's a lot more to this story than you know! Nothing is adding up, Brenda! This doesn't make any sense!"

"Mom, everything is adding the hell up." I was so angry with her. "Mom, what are you talking about? Joe had me feeling really bad. He was abusing me with all the mean things he said to me."

"Brenda, I know that Joe loves you! There is so much more to this story than you could even possibly realize now."

I immediately got pissed off at her. She was justifying Joe again. I read the entire letter that Joe had given to the girl to my mom, Lacey, and David. As I was reading it, the letter seemed off. It sounded like he was trying to plead with her. Lacey and David didn't have much to say.

Minutes later, Joe called David. David answered the phone outside. Joe said to David, "I couldn't get away from that girl. She threatened me all the time. If I didn't go over there, she said she would tell Brenda what I did." Joe asked David if I was okay and if he thought it would be okay if he came home.

David walked over to me with the phone in his hand. He tried to explain what Joe was voicing to him on the phone. David said, "Brenda, you have to be a little more understanding!"

I looked at David with the most disgusted look on my face. Now, I was crazy pissed. I screamed, "You all want me to be understanding? I am about sick of understanding him. Are you frickin' kidding me? I just found out that this bastard was cheating on me, and your stupid ass wants me to be understanding?"

What a stupid asshole, I thought. I did not listen to a word he said.

David quickly went back outside and told Joe that he did not think it would be a good idea for him to come home now. David said, "Brenda is not doing too well." Joe and David are more than just brothers-in-law. They're more like brothers. They have spent many years working together and have built a close bond.

Chapter 12

LATER THAT NIGHT, AFTER EVERYONE LEFT, THE GIRL CALLED MY cell phone again. She said, "I'm worried. Where is Joe?"

I said, "I don't know. I thought maybe he was with you."

She said, "No, he doesn't want me. He wants you."

I said, "Sister, you can have him. I don't want him."

She said, "What do you think he is going to do to me?"

I said, "I have no idea! All I do know is that he knows you messed up a good marriage. I don't blame you for telling me. I appreciate everything you said. Thank you for telling me. At least I know what I am married to and I now know what he is. It's just me finding out years later that he cheated. I will never be able to trust and forgive him. I know Joe and I will never work. Once a cheater, always a cheater. I'm leaving him!"

I asked her many questions that night. "Did you ever go out together?"

"No, we couldn't!"

"Did you go out to eat or to a movie?"

"No."

"Did he tell you he loved you?"

"Yeah."

I was so confused. I had felt Joe and I were in a better place in our marriage. Now craziness was in my mind. If I left him now, I wouldn't enjoy the fruits of all the hard work he did with Samantha. I kept thinking to myself, *You could have another baby right now! Thank God you terminated the pregnancy. Look what would've happened if you had decided to keep the baby. You would be on your own with four little kids to raise.* I stayed up all night, thinking and wondering about what I should do.

The next day, I had to work at home. I tried getting myself together enough to get up and move. I had the runs so bad. I called my boss and called out for the day.

Soon after, Joe walked through the door. He went into our bedroom to lie down on our bed, not saying anything to me. I was pissed.

I went in. "Are you going to tell me what the hell is going on?"

"Brenda, you don't understand. I tried to get away from that girl. She threatened me and said she was going to tell you."

"You think I'm some asshole? Why the hell didn't you let me leave you then? You got me pregnant twice after that! I had no idea you were out having fun sex with some frickin' girl, and then you'd come home to treat me like a piece of shit."

Joe said, "You would think like that. That's what my parents thought when I was going to the lake with the man who molested me. You don't understand! I only wanted to hurt myself. I wanted to hurt you so you could hurt me." Joe was crying hard. His face was completely red.

I couldn't understand what he was saying. His face looked as if it would burst at any second. In my world, sex was fun and felt good. His crying was out of control. I knew he liked to have sex with me.

Joe said, "Please, I already called Samantha. She will be able to explain everything to you."

I shook my head and walked out of the room.

Meanwhile, my mom called Joe's mom and told her everything that had happened. Joe's mom came over to our house. She already knew something was wrong.

Annette asked, "Brenda, are you okay?"

"Yeah, I'm okay," I said. "Can you do me a favor? Can you please watch the kids? Joe and I need to take a ride and talk."

"Sure. Go ahead. Go. The kids will be okay." Annette looked at Joe and gave him a nasty smirk. If facial expressions could speak, her smirk expressed how disappointed she was with him.

Annette and my mom became good friends. I also got closer with Annette. I learned to accept her on a deeper level. Annette and my mom came to our house just about every Friday night to watch our kids so Joe and I could go out for a few hours. It seemed the more I was able to open up to Annette, the more she opened up to me.

Joe and I left to talk. We got into the car. Joe said, "Don't you understand? I hated myself! I felt like a piece of shit."

I was screaming. "You took me down to the lowest place in my life. Look at what you made me do to Gracie! Look at all the shit you said to me. You used to scream at me. You don't love me! I can't feel love from you. All along, you were feeling love from some frickin' girl. You really are a piece of shit!"

"You don't know what that girl did to me. I hate that girl."

"You must have loved her then. And you're only saying you hate her because she ratted you out."

"Hell no!" he yelled. "I hated her way back then. I am glad and relieved you know now. I feel like a weight has been lifted off my shoulders. Please go with me. Let Samantha explain what that frickin' girl did to me. Brenda, she would not leave me alone. Please, just come with me."

Chapter 13

JOE AND I HAD PLANNED MONTHS BEFORE TO GO TO ATLANTIC City to see Aaron Lewis in concert. Joe and I have been going to his concerts for the past six years. Joe loves Aaron Lewis! He always said he could relate to all his music. I knew in my heart that the songs Joe so desperately wanted me to listen to were Joe's way of saying sorry to me—Joe's way of helping me understand him. A part of me did not want to go; another part of me needed to understand.

I went with Joe to the concert. We had front-row seats. From every single lyric to every song, I sat and listened. I remember one song's lyrics: "I'm on the outside. I'm looking in." I cried like a baby. Only then was I able to hear the reasons why Joe took me to these concerts. My crying was out of control. I was not ready to face these words, and I surely was not ready to understand Joe.

Within the next couple of days, I made plans to go away for a weekend with my friend Kim for her bachelorette party. My thoughts were strained. I fully intended to have sex with some random guy. I didn't care who it was.

For the bachelorette party, we went to a club in downtown Washington, DC. As we were walking around this extremely crowded club, someone I could not see tried to feel up my skirt, very hard and strong. I felt so violated. I was scared and angry. I looked around to see who had done it but couldn't spot the person. We were like sardines in there. Thank God the skirt I was wearing was not short but went to my knees.

This happened a few times as we were trying to move past the crowd. I felt very afraid and could not wait to sit down in a chair so this bastard wouldn't do it again. I told my friend Kim, but I didn't want to wreck her night. I stayed in the chair most of the night. I wanted to leave in the worst way, but I was so afraid to leave the girls I was with. I sat down near the bar and drank.

Many thoughts were running through my head. I knew I had wanted to have sex on the way here. Because of the asshole who kept trying to put his hand up my skirt, I didn't know what to think. With no idea who this person was, I wanted to catch him and punch him dead in the face. This experience completely changed my tune and way of thinking. I went into some kind of defense with everyone around me. I didn't trust anyone. I was constantly looking over my shoulder. We stayed at this club for a few hours and then went back to our hotel.

The next morning, we packed up the truck, stopped for breakfast, and drove home. Joe called me a few times throughout the night. I thought, *His only worry is to know what I will do here.*

Needless to say, Joe and I were not getting along. At the time, my behavior had changed drastically. I usually wore short skirts and heels with my hair done. I made sure I was looking pretty damn sexy. I felt as if I needed someone to help me feel good. I could not see anything good in Joe. I called him names all the time. I told him that I didn't love him. I often voiced to him, "I'm only using you for your money. I never loved you anyway." I even said, "I hate you."

He begged me to go talk to Samantha. I found myself going out to bars daily late at night for a beer or two. I needed to drink all the time. I went to local parks, searching for complete strangers to have sex with. My actions did not match my true character. I noticed that I was going against my own grain.

Joe kept trying to make things work between us. He voiced how much he loved me and said that he would never leave me. I told Joe I was talking to a guy at work and I really liked him. I said to Joe that I didn't want to be with him anymore—that I found this guy to be real with me. The guy didn't pressure me to be anything I wasn't. He talked to me as if he really cared for me. This guy was just a nice, average guy who was going to make me feel better.

But then again, I was playing with Joe's head. I allowed Joe to believe that I was going to make things better between us. I felt so mixed up. One day, I was trying to be with Joe; the next day, I would try to be with the other guy. At the time, I could not understand what I was feeling. Many people were telling me how nice my legs were and how smart and pretty I was. However, Joe was making dinner and cleaning the house, doing everything right.

One day, Joe and I went to see Samantha. Our session lasted two and a half hours. Samantha talked about the brain again and how it works. I sat and listened. I was thinking, *This woman is nuts! I cannot believe this lady is still talking about the damn brain and Joe's horrific feelings and thoughts.*

Samantha said, "I listened to a lot of the messages that girl left on Joe's phone. There were a few times that Joe and I spent entire sessions just listening to all the nasty, threatening messages she left him. When the girl called Joe, if he didn't respond, she'd act out with many text messages, threatening Joe that she would tell you to get what she wanted."

I was thinking, *This is just great. All of you are all nuts—you, Joe, and the girl! Each version of the story is worse than the last.*

After an hour and a half, midway through the session of Samantha talking about the brain and men being sexually abused as children, I asked her some questions. "Why didn't he leave me then?"

She said, "He never wanted to leave you."

"I wanted to leave him then," I said, "and I am pissed at you, Samantha, for not telling me. I think you should have told me what my husband was doing—you know, like woman to woman. Why didn't you tell me that my husband was having an affair with some girl? Why?"

"I couldn't do that. Joseph is my patient. But I did suggest for him to tell you many times so he didn't have to endure so much pain and horrific abuse."

"Well, why didn't he tell me?" I asked Samantha.

"He was afraid of losing you. Anyone else on this planet would have told you and given up. No one would have endured that much pain."

"So, let me ask you, who is the victim—the girl or Joe?"

"There are no victims in this! They both played their part. You are the only innocent one."

With Samantha saying "You're the only innocent one" to me, a defensive tone to my voice came to the surface; I immediately twisted the words *innocent* and *victim*. I said to Samantha, "Oh, no, I am not a victim! I will never be a victim! I did nothing wrong! I will get myself right, and I will come out the other side of this, with or without Joe. So please, Samantha, don't make me out to be a victim. Well, if Joe had a play in it, who was he?"

Samantha smirked. "Well, Brenda, he was a dirty dog! He was mostly the man who molested him. Joe often told the girl, 'Don't tell!' but he felt like the hurt little boy."

I shook my head. "I just cannot believe that I didn't leave him then. I cannot figure out why."

Samantha smiled and nodded.

"Samantha, there is no way in hell. I know for a fact that I would have left him then. I wanted to leave him anyway. I wanted to just because of the look in his eyes. If it weren't for my mother calling me every day, trying to make me understand him, I would have left. It's all my mother's fault! My mom talked me into staying with this asshole."

Samantha smiled and nodded. "Brenda, you may not want to hear this, but you and Joseph are the best couple on the block." I looked at her as if she was from Mars. She continued. "You're a very strong couple."

I thought, *This lady must have hit her head. She's nuts. I do not know where her mind is. All I know is that we are in danger. I have one foot out and half a foot in my marriage.* "Do you really think you're going to smooth over Joe's affair?" I said.

Samantha smiled. "I cannot tell you what to do." Samantha then said to Joe, "Joseph, the horrific feelings you held on to as a young boy do not give you an excuse to have an affair."

Joe nodded. "I know. I know. I don't want Brenda to feel sorry for me."

I yelled with an angry tone to my voice, "Feel sorry for you! Oh, no, I don't feel sorry for you, you frickin' asshole. I hate you! The only thing I'm sorry for is that I even married you!"

Samantha said, "Brenda, Joe tried early on to end it."

I said, "Now don't you go and blame this girl. It is not her fault. Joe is the one I am married to. I don't care what that damn girl did to him."

Samantha said, "Brenda, you could never have given Joseph what he needed at that time. This sex was not a fun, enjoyable thing for Joseph. He endured horrific abuse as a child and chose to work with me to overcome it. He now has tools. You said it yourself; Joseph is a better man now."

"Yeah, but I didn't know he was cheating on me. What should I do, Samantha? If I leave him now, I will not enjoy the fruits of all the work he did with you." Samantha nodded. I looked over at Joe. I asked him, "Just what did this man do to you anyway?"

Samantha quickly spoke over my words with a strong tone in her voice. She looked at Joe. "Joseph, the story—your story—does not matter! You do not need to share the details of your story with Brenda or anyone else. I would recommend to you that you do not tell Brenda at this time. Maybe in time—give it a year or two. I highly recommend you do not tell her now." Samantha leaned over to Joe. "You're finished with crisis therapy."

I gave them both a look, like, *I deserve to know what that man did to him.* I did not believe Joe was real with me. I wanted Joe to tell me what that man did to him when he was a little boy. I felt as though he owed it to me. Joe told me some things the man did to him. But I always pushed for more. Nothing Joe said seemed good enough. Joe always stopped when he was trying to talk about what had happened to him as a child.

He said, "I'm trying, but I don't feel right. I just don't feel right."

With a sad look in his eyes, I heard the importance in Samantha's voice when she said, "Your story does not matter."

Chapter 14

*I*FELT VERY VULNERABLE; I WENT TO LOCAL PARKS AND SAT THERE in my truck to prey upon nice-looking men. I drank every chance I got. I felt as if I couldn't get enough. I was still leaning on the guy at work and told him all that Joe had done to me. I wanted this guy, but then I would also have sex with Joe just about every single day.

I was so confused, still voicing negative things to Joe: "I don't love you. I am only with you for your money. I never wanted to marry you. I hate you." I called him a piece of shit. I felt alone, like the biggest scumbag on earth. I said all these negative words to Joe, and then I wanted to take them back after I said them. I meant, "This is what you were, not now." Then I'd have sex with him and then say, "I think you're good now."

He said, "Brenda, I just want you to be happy. I don't want you to stay with me if you don't love me. I don't want you to feel sorry for me, Brenda. But you are doing the same things I did to you. I didn't understand I was in a depression. Samantha explained everything to you. Why do you keep treating me like a piece of shit?"

"You treated me like shit. You looked like you hated me."

"But I hated myself," he said. "I wanted you to hate me so I could hate myself. Brenda, I'd die for you. I love you so much. Look at all the work I did to become a better person for you. I didn't know what was wrong with me. That was not fun for me. You're thinking it was fun, but it wasn't."

"Joe, that's what I feel like now. I don't believe you are real! I'm so confused I need someone to help me feel better."

Joe was still always trying to get me to eat. I lost about fifteen to twenty pounds during this time. The thought of food made me sick. I could not eat. I constantly had the runs.

One day, I was on my way to my office, and I stopped for coffee at Wawa, the "pickup place." A few men were there at the counter, making their coffee. They started flirting with me. I put my head down and walked away.

As I got into the office, it seemed as if everyone I looked at said something nice to me: "Wow, Brenda! You really lost a lot of weight. You look awesome. You're so sexy. You have beautiful legs. You're gorgeous, girl."

Close friends knew why. I told some friends about the abortion. At first, I told them just to be real. But on this day, I was getting way too much attention from everyone in all directions. It seemed like I could not make these people stop giving me positive attention. I just wanted them all to stop. Everyone thought I was a great person, but on the inside, my feelings were the complete opposite. I tried hard to cover my thoughts and feelings.

My boss, Ashley, asked me to come into her office for my yearly review. When I went into her office, Ashley asked, "How are you?"

I said, "Well."

She started her review. She said all the same positive things she had always said the last nineteen years. As she was telling me how great I was, I felt myself busting. Every single word that came out of her mouth made me feel twenty times worse.

"Please, please, can you just stop?" I was trying not to cry. "Just give me the paper to sign so I can get out of here." I could not take another word out of her mouth.

"Are you okay?"

"Yeah, I'm okay. I just need to get out of here."

I signed the paper, slid it across the desk, and left her office. I could not understand why I had acted like that with her. Nothing she had said was negative. I love her to death. She is the best manager anyone could ever ask for. She was saying all these nice things to me. However, I had wanted to reach over the table, choke her, and scream, "Don't you frickin' get it? I am the biggest piece of shit on this earth. I just killed a beautiful little baby. Don't you get that? I'm not that great person you think I am! I am a piece of shit!"

I went back to my desk, grabbed my stuff, and went to lunch. I sat in my car, crying, and wrote a letter to Joe. I wrote down just what had happened. It was painful for me to get it out. I felt like the biggest piece of shit.

I could not feel the physical pain in my side anymore. I thought, *I could have had that baby. I could have dealt with the pain. The pain wasn't that bad. It would only have been nine months. I am such a piece of shit. What kind of person does that to her baby?* After writing down all I was feeling, I started to feel a little better. I went back to the office and continued working.

After work, I went to my parents' house. Both my parents were there. I walked in. The first words to my dad were, "I had an abortion!" I wanted him to tell me what a piece of shit I was. I wanted to see his reaction. I said, "Yeah, I killed a little baby. I feel like a piece of shit."

My dad said, "Well, come sit down. Sometimes in life, we do things that we cannot take back." He started talking about all the really horrific things he saw in the Vietnam War. He said, "I remember getting off the plane in Vietnam. I remember seeing a sign that read 'Bodies go here.' I remember my friends dying, and US Marines would drag their bodies under the sign and leave them there. I lost so many good friends who got their legs amputated. This one woman hated me! We had just bombed her house with her family and kids in it. I could never get her look out of my mind. This lady hated me with pure disgust in her eyes."

"Oh my God, Dad, I know exactly what you're talking about. When I went to get the abortion, a priest was outside the clinic. He looked at me the same exact way. I can't seem to get that man's look out of my mind."

My mom sat and listened to us talk. My dad and I were crying for most of our conversation. I felt a huge sense of relief in my chest. I knew my dad really understood what I was saying to him. It was like we both felt the same exact way. We both had done something that we could never, ever take back, and we understood we were both there to listen to each other's life experiences.

That day was really a life-changing one for me. I felt so grateful for my dad. He had really helped me when I needed it most. I went home and wrote a letter about having an abortion and my dad's experiences in war—how our stories are so different but the feelings are alike.

I had a few friends who chose to have abortions, for whatever reason. I thought my letter could possibly help others. I decided to post the letter as a note on Facebook. I was completely blown away by the feedback from women who said it had helped them with their stories. I had many messages expressing women's stories and reasons behind them. I wanted to help them with their feelings.

I realized there are many men and women suffering from their own pain, not able to understand the reasons why they feel it. The awareness and this realization helped me get in touch with what I was feeling inside. I understood why I was acting out and seeking out men; the urge to drink alcohol diminished.

I felt closer to Joe. I told him about the guy at work and explained to him why I had done that. I explained my feelings to him and the reasons why I had acted like that. Joe said he understood. Joe felt as if he was to blame for all my thoughts.

I asked Joe, "Do you think you will be able to forgive me?"

Joe said, "Absolutely."

As I started to feel and see a better version of myself, I realized that every single feeling, thought, and action of mine had nothing to do with Joe. It was always about me and my feelings at the time. Joe had had the same kind of feelings prior to me; however, I was the one who had become them.

I started to feel alive. I sat down and wrote a beautiful letter to Joe. It took ten to twenty minutes for me to write it. As I was writing this letter, I felt electric under my skin. My hands felt very powerful. I knew Joe would understand every single word in the letter. My heart could finally understand that everything Samantha had said to me was 100 percent true. I felt so much power within myself that I had not yet discovered or learned to accept. I'd never in my life felt so grateful for everyone around me—my parents, Joe, and Samantha. I felt as if I was on top of a mountain.

I spoke to my mom on the phone every day. I explained everything I had learned. For all of Joe's pain, I could now completely understand and forgive him. I read the letter to my mom first. She begged me to give it to him that day.

I said, "No, I'm going to wait until Father's Day. That's when I'm going to give it to him."

My mom said, "I just can't wait for him to get that letter. He is going to love it."

I felt so grateful and so much joy, complete and happy inside. I learned so much about myself. I learned every single thing in my life had happened for a reason. I felt something greater in my heart. I am not the best secret keeper. I wanted to give the letter to Joe in the worst way.

Annette and my mom were coming over so Joe and I could go out to dinner and have some alone time, just the two of us.

My mom knew about the letter. "Maybe you will give Joe the letter tonight!"

"No, Mom, I'm waiting for Father's Day," I said, but I was feeling so anxious to see Joe's reaction.

Later, we came home after a great night. We sat and talked to our moms for a while. When they left, Joe and I went to bed. We started playing around with each other. We made love like never before. I felt as if I wanted to climb into his body.

Joe said, "Oh my God! Oh my God!" His whole body trembled as he was climaxing. He had never felt so good in all his life. Also, for the very first time, we felt equal. He showed me every feeling he had inside. I returned all that he showed me. We felt as one. It was the perfect time for me to give Joe his letter. I got up, dressed, ran to my truck, and got his letter.

As he read it, he started to cry. "You wrote this all by yourself?"
I said, "Yeah."
"No one helped you?"

"No. This letter took about ten minutes to write, and I mean every word of it."

Joe said, "This feels like a dream. This is the best present anyone has ever given me. I love this, Brenda. It means the world to me."

We lay in our bed and cried, feeling joy. We were truly connected in every possible way. We lay there for about an hour.

I got this overwhelming feeling again. I felt so much energy in my hands. I jumped up out of bed at around two in the morning, thinking, *Oh my God, I need to write to the powerful lady. Without her, none of this would be possible.*

Again, as I wrote the words down on paper, I felt electric under my skin. I completely understood every single word that she had said to me. She knew I needed to hear them. I was pissed at her; however, I also found Samantha to be the most powerful person in my life. I had many aha moments.

I felt as if I would never be able to thank her enough. But then again, I thought, *You bitch, you understood all of this all along? You knew the feelings we were dealing with. You allowed us to feel every single negative feeling as individuals so we could reach for peace and live in this happy, loving place as individual people. Oh my God—therefore, our marriage could become what it is today.* My writing felt so powerful in my hands.

Without this powerful lady, I'd never understand. I could never feel this good inside—this true appreciation to have such a powerful woman in my life. I couldn't believe it. Not only did she help Joe, but she guided me through my own depression.

I now know Samantha is a very powerful gift to Joe and myself. She changed our lives. We are better people. We are a better couple. We are better human beings. She has spread her love into us. I instinctively knew she had felt her own pain to become the powerful woman she was today. I could feel the miracle of overcoming myself. I knew she felt the same for herself.

Every single feeling I felt had absolutely nothing to do with Joe and his affair. I had found out about the affair at that time, so I had a reason to place blame. I wrote exactly what I needed to say to Samantha. I gave the letter to Joe to read and rewrite the final copy. We framed the letter together.

The next day, Joe called to make an appointment with her, allowing Samantha to believe Joe was the only one coming. As we drove to Samantha's office, Joe and I were filled with pure appreciation for her. We took our kids along with us. Joe went into her office first and gave Samantha the letter I had given to him. They both came out crying. They came out to get us.

I handed Samantha the letter meant for her. "Thank you so much for all you have done for us. You truly are a very powerful gift to us."

Samantha sat, read our letter, and cried. She was so happy that we had stuck it out. She said again, "You and Joseph are the best couple on the block. Your gift is your story."

I smiled and could finally accept what she was telling us.

Samantha asked, "This is from both of you?"

I said, "Yeah, it's my words and Joe's handwriting." We had not felt the need to type her letter. We wanted her to see the humanness in the words within it.

Samantha said, "Can I hang this in my office for my patients to read?"

Joe and I looked at each other. Without any hesitation, we said, "Sure. We would love that."

Samantha said, "That's great, but your names are written on it. Do you want to take it home and remove your names?"

I said, "No. Every single word that is written in this note is exactly how it was. I am not ashamed of it. I wish that this hopefully helps other couples with their own stories."

She sat back in her chair and smiled with tears in her eyes. As Joe and I were leaving Samantha's office, we repeatedly thanked her for all she had done for us.

Driving home, our kids Joseph and Gracie asked us questions. "Who was that lady?"

I smiled. "That lady helped us understand each other."

Gracie asked, "Why was she crying?"

I said, "She's happy to see Daddy and Mommy so happy together."

I felt as though nothing or no one would ever hurt us. Joe and I had discovered another mountaintop. Everything in our life was perfectly imperfect. Everything I saw was full of happiness.

When we got home, I called my mom and told her all about our trip to Samantha's office. My mom said, "You and Joe both need to thank God for her. She has done so much for both of you. You two would never be able to understand all that you have been through if you hadn't had her in your life."

I completely agreed with every word my mom said. We talked for hours about Samantha. I explained to my mom that Samantha had her own pain. She had to suffer to become the woman she is today and do the kind of work she does.

Chapter 15

*T*IME WENT ON. AS I WAS TELLING MORE PEOPLE MY STORY, I FELT empowered. My sole purpose was to help others understand their stories. I felt that I could help them understand themselves. I had felt many horrific feelings. I understood why we were all on our journeys— possibly self-destructive paths. I felt the need to help everyone around me. I wanted everyone to be happy and know what it was like to actually feel true love.

I talked to many friends, trying my hardest to get them to understand what their own feelings were. Feelings have a major impact on our thoughts and actions. I talked and talked to them, but it seemed as though they could not hear what I was saying. In addition, they were not willing to make changes in their lives.

I asked myself, *It seems so easy to understand. Why are they not getting it? Why are they not using what I am saying to them and applying it to their lives? Why can't they see it? Why can't they get it?*

One day, I was talking to my mom on the telephone. I was explaining the way to love, just as it happened to me. It was just as I saw it. I was trying too hard to get her to understand. I felt like a know-it-all type of person. I felt completely right, like I was the only person on earth who had found this place of being. I had such a need to get as many people to feel this as possible.

After I got off the phone with her, something happened. I felt as though I was outside my body. I tried like hell to get back in. I did not know what was wrong with me. I felt completely out of my mind. I got back in; I didn't tell anyone what had happened because they'd never believe me.

This happened a few times in a few weeks. Each time, I felt as if I could not get back into my body. As this happened more and more, each time, I heard a voice. I was not in my body. It scared the crap out of me. I felt extremely crazy and completely panicked.

I ran all over my house. I did not know what to do or how to control this voice. I just wanted this voice to stop. I knew it was powerful. Oh my, I was extremely afraid, and I didn't want any part of it. The best word to describe what happened is *horrifying.* I've been alive for thirty-five years. In all my days, I had never felt that I was out of my body, not to mention hearing an unknown voice. The weirdest thing: I felt happiness, joy, and love inside. Yet I was still crazy, horrified in the process—very alone, wanting to control it. My instinct knew this would not stop or leave me alone until I allowed it to happen. I was not going to fight this anymore. *Whatever it is, it is!* I thought.

When my spirit was outside my body, I did not even try to get it back in. I felt ready to hear whatever this voice had to say. Now all I heard was "I'm giving you this gift. Teach with it!" I believed I knew who it was.

I reached as high as I could go. There was no one around to help me—that is, no one with the true feeling of love who knew me. I am not a religious person. I did not go to church. The only prayer I have ever said is "Thank you." I could not tell anyone this had happened. Also, I could not wrap my head around this voice: "I'm giving you this gift. Teach with it." That was all I heard. I didn't see anything or any light of any kind. All I was capable of doing was listening.

The experience didn't feel normal to me, so I set up an appointment with Samantha, someone I knew in my heart I had a connection with. She had discovered love within herself.

I went into her office, still embarrassed, alone, crazy, and angry. I started talking frantically. I asked her questions about herself. Already knowing her answers, I asked, "You discovered love for yourself, right?"

She said, "Yes."

"Does everyone find this?"

"Yes, some do."

"I felt like I was not in my body."

"That can happen when we are scared, horrified, or panicked."

"Listen, Samantha, I heard a man's voice." I did not want to tell her. I repeatedly said, "I know I'm crazy. I'm crazy." I said, "Samantha, I know this sounds crazy." I started to cry. I explained I felt as if I was out of my body, still crying.

Samantha asked, "Were you panicked?"

"Yeah, I could not get back in. I tried, and I kept hearing this voice."

"Who?"

"Him." I felt very alone, along with shame and anger. "I know I'm crazy! This is not normal."

"Who?"

"You know him. Did he ever talk to you?"

"Who?"

With much hesitation, I said, "You know, God. See, I know I'm nuts. This is not normal. I did not want him to talk to me. I don't know why he picked me. I'm not educated. I don't know anything. I hope he does not come to me again. That was scary. That was sure not what you think it would be. Samantha, please tell me I am nuts. I know I am nuts. I know this is not normal. What should I do? I cannot tell anyone this. They'd never believe me anyway. I told Joe. He probably thinks I'm nuts. What am I going to do? Please, Samantha, please tell me what to do. You are the only person I can feel found love from within.

"I don't know Oprah Winfrey. I only know she feels this way because of her words and what she does for the world. I have no connection with her. She does not know me. I don't have a real connection with anyone. Everyone needs to feel this way. I can see their pain in their eyes. They just don't understand yet! I want them to feel this way, same as you and me. I need them to learn how to feel it.

"What am I going to do? I've tried everything I can think of to get my family and friends to see what they're missing. I know that it's just not the right time for some. Why does it take time? I need all to find this place of love right now. This is not fair. Why do I get to see this great place? Why I am feeling so great and everyone else is doing drugs or drinking or hiding behind their egos? Their pain will never go away until they face it. They need to know where they're at. Samantha, when I look into their eyes, I can see their pain. When they speak to me, I hear their pain. It hurts me really bad. All I want to do is pull it out of them so they don't have to carry it anymore. I think I can do it."

Samantha nodded and smiled.

I asked, "Did you ever see the movie *The Green Mile?*"

She smiled.

"You know he's real! I feel like him. I feel people's pain like he does. You know how he takes the cancer out of the woman's mouth? I think I can help remove people's feelings."

Again, Samantha smiled.

"I need to find a way to help these people. They don't know any better. All they know is what they're feeling. It is impossible to truly know what you're feeling if we are not open to the feeling. I need them to know I felt like the lowest person on the planet. I know that God forgave me for everything I did. They all can do it too. I wouldn't understand this if I didn't have you in my life."

Samantha just sat there smiling.

"Look, they may not believe me because I'm not educated. I do not have the statistics like you do. Maybe they just yes me to death. They all say I am right. I don't want to hear I'm right. I want them to look into themselves and find their own purposes. I don't have time to go back to school with three kids and a full-time job just to find out all I have already felt and lived. I could never find this knowledge in a damn textbook. I don't need school. I've lived every single negative feeling there is for me to feel to reach this being, my true self. And now that I've found this other side, I can use the tools you gave me to climb my way back up if I need to fall. Maybe I needed to hear those words for encouragement. You know, I do not know the reason. All I do know is I am going to teach just like he told me to do."

Samantha smiled.

"All the pain of my past brought me to this very spot. I needed every single bit of it to discover the woman I am today."

Samantha smiled. My session was over. Again, I thanked her for listening.

Chapter 16

$\mathcal{M}$Y MOM AND ANNETTE CAME OVER THAT NIGHT TO WATCH OUR kids as they had been doing for the past year. My mom wanted Joe and me to leave. We didn't have anything planned. We wanted to sit and talk with her. My mom told us to go to the movies and get something to eat.

She said, "You guys go on now. I want to spend time with the kids." As Kathryn was lying on her lap, my mom was running her hand through her curly hair.

Joe and I left. As we were driving to the movies, I said to Joe, "Something is not right with my mom."

Joe said, "She has a lot of shit on her mind."

"I know, but something really isn't right with her. She seems off."

"Brenda, she has a lot of stress in her life."

"She has always had stress in her life."

When Joe and I went home, we sat and talked to her for a bit. Then she left. My mother had been diagnosed with diabetes about a year before. She had a difficult time seeing, especially at night.

I said, "Please just stay here. You can sleep in Gracie's room."

My mom said, "No, I've got to go home and make sure your dad has something to eat."

My dad had been diagnosed with chronic lymphocytic leukemia about ten years before, a direct link to Agent Orange in Vietnam. He had rounds of chemotherapy; he has been cancer-free since. My mom worried about my dad all the time. She made sure he was always taken care of. She made him dinner every night and cut up his food.

My parents still lived in the same home that I was raised in, a small row home with one bathroom upstairs. My mom worried about how she'd take care of him if he was to be bedridden. Their home was not accommodating, with steps going into their home. The bedrooms were upstairs. Now that we kids were grown and living on our own, she was financially stable to remodel their home.

I said, "Mom, just do it!" I wanted her to enjoy whatever made her happy. My brothers, David and Eddie, and Joe helped with the work.

A few weeks later, my mom called Joe and asked what he thought it would cost to remodel the kitchen. Mom said she would call a guy named Steve and get a price from him and call the cabinet guy and get a price. She got estimates on appliances, floor, paint, and so forth. She decided to do it.

David and Joe knocked out the walls and gutted the whole downstairs. The remodel was done within a few weeks. The house was completed just the way she always dreamed. Mom loved her new kitchen. I helped her decorate. I was so happy for her. She finally got what she always talked about.

When I was a little girl, my mom talked about remodeling our house all the time. Her story never changed. It always started the same: "When I get the money, it will be one room at a time. When I get the money, I am going to get a new bow window. I am going to knock out that wall between the kitchen and dining room. I'm going to get a new kitchen with French doors to lead out back."

She talked about the house often, to the point that I got sick of listening. She said exactly the way she wanted it. Everything she talked about all those years, my mom finally got it. She could not wait to have Christmas dinner with all of us kids and grandchildren together, all able to fit in the same room.

Some time passed. My mom started to become distant with me. In the past, I had talked to her just about every single day of my life on the telephone. Sometimes, it was a couple of times a day. Now when she called me, she asked about the kids and then got me off the phone. I could sense something was not right with her.

I asked her several times, "What is wrong, Mom? Are you okay? You're not acting right. What's bothering you?" We always had the kind of relationship that we could tell each other everything and anything. However, something was definitely changing. I knew she was keeping something from me. But I couldn't put my finger on it.

My mom came over every Friday night to babysit. She started to keep the conversations between us brief. She came over a few times during the week just to go into my bedroom to sleep. Now I knew something was really wrong. She didn't want to even be in my company. When I asked her so many times what was wrong, she would say, "I just have the flu. I'm okay. I'm fine. I can't call the doctor for antibiotics. I'm allergic."

Weeks passed. My sister, Tara, and David both lived in the same town as my parents. They stopped at her house often.

Tara said, "Brenda, all she's doing is sleeping and coughing. She's not calling anyone back. Her friends want her to go to the doctor. She's not even answering the phone anymore."

My mom was always on the phone. She had so many childhood friends.

Tara said, "Something is wrong with Mommy. Her coughing is getting bad. Brenda, you need to do something. You need to talk her into going to the hospital."

I went over to my mom's house that night, along with David and Eddie. We begged her to go to the doctor.

My mom said, "Look, I know me. I am fine. I'm going to give it a couple more days. If I don't get better, I'll go. But until then, leave me the hell alone. I just want to be left alone. I'm fine. I'm an adult. I can take care of myself. I do not need you to tell me what I need to do. I know what I'm doing." Meanwhile, as she was trying to talk, her coughing worsened, and it became difficult for her to breathe.

Days passed. She was not getting out of bed. She turned the ringer off on her phone, which she had never done.

Her friend Kelly called me. She told me how bad my mom needed to go to the doctor. She said, "I just left your mom's house, and we got into a fight because she's not listening."

"Kelly, I know what you mean. Tara, David, and I tried to get her to go too. But she won't. Listen, Kelly, I am afraid for her to go to the doctor. I'm afraid of what they're going to tell her. I need her to go, but I don't want her to."

Kelly said, "Your goddamn mother is a pain in my ass! Me, Leanne, and Joyce have been on her to go to the doctor. She is not answering our calls. Brenda, you really need to make her go."

Therefore, I drove over to my mom's house. She was coughing constantly. I said, "Mom, you're going to call the doctor now while I'm here."

She finally agreed and called the doctor's office. I waited to hear what they had to say. They made her appointment for the next day.

The next day, my mother went to her appointment. They listened to her chest and told her that she had pneumonia in both lungs and needed to go to the hospital for them to treat her. I was unable to go to her doctor's appointment. I told her to call me when she was done. When Mom got home, she called to tell me what had happened. She said, "I have pneumonia."

I said, "Really, that's all? That's good. I'm glad that's all it is, Mom. I'll be right over to take you to the hospital."

I got Kathryn and myself dressed. I picked my mom up at her house. As we were driving to the hospital, I said, "Mom, I was really scared. I thought maybe whatever you had was so much worse than it is. I don't know how you are doing it. I only had a touch of pneumonia, and I was sick as a dog. I had a high fever and the sweats too!"

When we arrived at the hospital, my sister met us there. My mom looked like she was in bad shape. When the doctor came in, my mom started telling him what issues she was having. The whole time, she was still coughing.

The doctor asked, "Have you been eating?"

My mom said, "Not really. I really don't have an appetite."

"Have you lost any weight?"

"Yeah, I lost a few pounds."

I stepped in and started talking over her. "Um, Doctor, she's lost about twenty-five to thirty pounds within the last few months. Her coughing is really bad."

The doctor nodded at me. "Have you had a fever?" he asked my mom.

She said, "No, I'm good."

"Do you smoke?"

She looked up and smirked. "Yeah." And she put her head back down.

The doctor said, "I'm going to order a chest X-ray."

Mom nodded at him. She then put her head down and started twiddling her thumbs. She never looked over at me or Tara. Then the X-ray tech came to get her.

Tara and I waited for Mom to come back. About a half hour later, they brought her back to the room. She was still lying there with her head down, twiddling her thumbs.

A few minutes later, the doctor came in and asked to speak with Tara and me in another room. We went in and sat down. He said, "I have bad news for you. Your mother has lung cancer. We found a large tumor on her right lung. Your mother has had this for at least two years."

Tara became completely hysterical.

I yelled, "Stop it! Get yourself together real quick. It's not about you." As I completed that sentence, I became a complete mess—hysterical, out of control. Oh my God, I could not gather my thoughts. I was crying out of control.

Shortly after, the doctor asked, "Do you want to go in while I tell her the news?"

We both said, "Yes."

A part of me didn't want to go into her room as the doctor told my mom. I squatted down on my feet so my mom could not see me.

The doctor walked into the room first. He walked over to my mother's bed and grabbed her hand. "Mrs. Whitaker, I'm sorry to tell you this, but you have a large tumor on your right lung."

My mom looked down at her hands and nodded.

"It's big and in a bad spot, but it may be treatable. I am not supposed to say this, but if you were my mother or loved one, I would have you at

Fox Chase Cancer Center, a place that specializes in cancer. This is not the right place for you." My mom smiled and nodded. He talked briefly with her and gave her a breathing treatment. The doctor said it would not make any difference to wait and go to a specialty hospital.

My mom said, "My husband goes to Fox Chase pretty often for checkups. I am familiar with some of the doctors there. Maybe they will recommend a good doctor for me."

The doctor said to her, "Mrs. Whitaker, I wish you all the best." He shook all our hands and left the room.

I asked, "Mom, are you okay? You can cry. Tara and I got it out in the other room. It's okay. I think you should cry!"

My mom looked up at Tara and me. With a really calm voice, she said, "I'm really sorry you had to find out this way. I've known this for a while. I just didn't have the heart to tell you." After she said that, we felt we had gotten our mom back. She looked right at us. She said, "Everything will be okay. Now that you know, I feel much better."

I asked, "Mom, you knew this?"

"Yeah."

"That's why you didn't want to talk to us."

"Yeah."

We gathered all her belongings to go home. We got into the car.

I said to my mom, "You're going to need to cry! Mom, it is okay. Why don't we sit here for a little while and cry? That way, you can get it out before you tell Daddy and the boys."

She said, "Brenda, I don't need to cry. I've known about this for a while. You are just finding this out now. It's much harder on you than it is me. I've had the time to think about this. You all haven't."

I didn't know whether to be pissed off at her for knowing all this time or to kiss and hug her because she was only trying to save us the pain of hearing she had cancer. We drove to my mom's house. My dad and brothers were there.

We walked in. I told them the troubled news. My mom sat in her chair, as if she finally had nothing to hide. My dad and brother were upset. I couldn't handle it, so I took a walk. I walked and walked and walked. I called Joe. I was screaming at him. "She is going to die. I know it! I know she is going to die, Joe! I just know it. I can feel it."

Joe tried to calm me down. "Brenda, just come home. I don't want you walking around like this."

I asked, "Are you nuts? Did you hear what I just said to you? My mother is dying!" I was completely out of control, crying hysterically. As I was walking, my hands were moving all over the place. Eventually, I felt calm enough to go back to my parents' house. I walked in with my head down.

My mom said, "Look, you." She pointed at me.

I asked, "What?"

"You have a vacation booked. You are going to get on that plane. You have kids that are excited to go. I will be really pissed off if you don't get on that plane." She said all this with a very demanding tone in her voice.

I said, "Mom, there is no way I'm going on that vacation."

"Brenda, all I have to say to you is that you'd better get on that plane."

I went over to her and hugged her. "I love you. I'll see you when I get back." I went home.

As I approached our house, Joe and his cousin Maria came up to greet me. They walked up to me and hugged me, both in tears. I was still crying. I said, "Maria, there is no way I can get on a plane after my mother was just diagnosed with lung cancer. I just can't do it."

Joe said, "Your mom is not that kind of person, Brenda. She wants you to go and have fun with the kids. There's nothing you can do for her."

I felt like a real asshole. *How am I going to go on vacation to Arizona when my mother is in this condition?* I thought. I called her house. I let all my kids talk and leave her a message.

I got on the phone last and told her how much I loved her. "I love you, Mom! We will see you when we get home."

Chapter 17

THE NEXT MORNING, WE LEFT FOR ARIZONA. A PART OF ME WANTED to go; another part of me wanted to be with my mom. I kept trying to justify going. I knew after I got on the plane that something was not right.

We landed in Arizona. The kids were super excited. We vacationed in Arizona at least twice a year as a family. Joe's stepbrother, Mike, and his wife, Linda, lived out there. We looked forward to hanging out with them.

The first couple of days went okay. I called and talked to my mother. She didn't seem distant with me at all. I tried to get her off the phone. I could hear her struggling voice. I could hear her breathing. She tried hard not to cough. I needed to hear her voice. I needed to know she was safe.

My mom's friends took her to a satellite hospital, Fox Chase Cancer Center. Her breathing and coughing had become horrific. The hospital admitted her. That day, there was an earthquake in Pennsylvania. I felt my mom was dying. I searched for flights to come home but could not find anything. I spoke to my sister and brother every day.

They said, "Brenda, she really isn't doing well. I think she is waiting for you to come home."

I felt the same way. I kept thinking how messed up this was. First, I even went on this vacation. Second, now my mother was actually waiting for me to come home so she could die. I knew in my heart that she was waiting for me. I could feel it. I cried a lot that day. I felt alone. I spent a lot of time on the floor in the hotel's laundry room.

Joe tried to keep me busy and talked me through it. That day, I felt hopeless. I tried to search for flights. But my mind couldn't think. I could not stay focused on anything.

The next day, Pennsylvania had a bad storm. All the phones were down, and I was at my lowest point. I cried to Joe. My words were hard for me to get out. I cried, "I just need to get home. I need to be there for her. I cannot believe this is happening. What happens if she dies and I am not there? I will never be able to live with myself! My family probably does not believe that there are no flights. They probably think I'm having a great time."

I just wanted to say, "Hello, Mom." I needed to see her. I needed to talk to her. I said, "Joe, please help me get to her."

"Brenda, listen. I checked. I'm really sorry, but no planes are landing at the Philadelphia airport."

"What am I going to do?" We were both crying. My phone rang constantly. Many people were calling.

Joe said, "Look, I'm trying to help you. You are driving yourself nuts. You keep answering the damn phone. You're listening to all these frickin' people. You need to stop answering the phone. The only calls you should be accepting are the hospital calls. Brenda, I will check first thing tomorrow morning. If there are any flights, I will get you there."

In the midst of us talking, I got a text message from my cousin Brianna. It said, "Call me!" with her phone number.

I called her back. We talked about me not being able to get home.

She said, "Look for flights in the surrounding area. My dad will pick you up wherever. You just need to get here fast."

"I know. I know. I need to get there!"

I told Joe to check all the surrounding airports. He found an overnight flight for the next day into Washington, DC, and booked it for me. I felt so much relief. I called Uncle Charles to ask if the location would be okay.

He said, "I know the area. I'm used to driving long distances."

"Oh my God, Uncle Charles, thank you so much!" I said. "You do not know how much I appreciate this. I don't know what I would do if it weren't for you picking me up."

Later that night, we met Mike and Linda for dinner. I felt really close to them.

Mike asked me, "Have you prepared yourself for your mom dying? Are you going to be okay?"

"Honestly, Mike, I am just trying to hold myself together. All I want is to be there with her. That is all I can think about. I am about to lose my mind here."

"Brenda, I want you to know that it's going to be really rough for you flying back there by yourself."

"I don't care about that!" I said. "I just need to be with my mother. Mike, she is like God to me! She helped me through so much in my life. I don't know what I'm going to do without her." I started crying.

"Brenda, we just want you to know that Linda and I love you. We are here for you! If you ever need us, we're here."

"I know. I know. Thank you so much!" I smiled at Mike.

After dinner, we went home. I packed all my stuff. I had to tell my kids. They knew something was wrong with me, and I didn't want them to feel like I was holding anything from them. Joseph and Gracie knew my mom was sick and in the hospital, but they did not know she was dying. After I packed, I had a talk with them.

I said, "You guys know my mom is sick, right?"

They said, "Yeah."

I said, "My mom is really sick and in pain. I need to go be with her in the hospital. I'm going to be leaving tomorrow so I can spend extra time with her."

Joseph asked, "Is she going to die?"

"I'm not 100 percent sure, but I think so." With tears in my eyes, I said, "Guys, I'm really sorry that I have been a mess on this trip. But my mom is really not doing well."

Gracie and Joseph looked so sad. They didn't say much, but I could see it in their eyes.

"You guys are going to be home in just two more days. You can come straight to the hospital as soon as you get off the plane."

They said, "Okay, Mom."

"Help Daddy with Kathryn. Help Daddy with the bags in the airport."

They said, "We will. We will be okay."

I called the hospital for the test results of her lungs. The doctor said that her lungs were extremely diseased, besides the large tumor and two small tumors on the right lung.

I asked, "How was my mother last night?"

The nurse asked, "Who are you?"

I said, "My name is Brenda. I'm her daughter. I'm the one who is stuck in Arizona."

She said, "Oh, yes, your mom has been talking about you."

I felt like the biggest loser. This was not the nurse I usually spoke to. I thought, *She probably thinks I'm some asshole not caring about my mom.*

The nurse asked, "Is there any way you can come home? She is calling for you."

I said, "I know. I am doing everything in my power to get there. I have a flight, and I will be there tomorrow afternoon."

"We started her on morphine. Your dad has talked to hospice. They made a decision."

"What do you mean? What decision?"

"Have you talked to your family?"

"Yeah, they didn't say anything about decisions."

"I'm sorry. I cannot give you personal information. You need to speak to your family members. All I can tell you is that a decision has been made."

Now I was full-blown frustrated. It was late Arizona time, three hours behind Pennsylvania. I didn't know who to call at that hour. I asked again, with a frustrated tone to my voice, "Who made the decision?"

The nurse said, "Your mother," with a stern tone to her voice.

"Well, that's fine. That's all you needed to tell me."

Chapter 18

THE NEXT DAY, I WAS IN A LOT BETTER SHAPE. MY HEAD WAS OKAY. I enjoyed my kids as much as possible. After dinner, Joe and the kids dropped me off at the airport. I kissed them all and told them that I loved them.

Joe said, "I will call you when we get back to the room."

"Okay," I said and smiled at him.

At the terminal, while waiting for my flight, I got an overwhelming urge to write. I felt a tingling sensation in my hands. Every bone in my body knew my mother was dying. I sat there and wrote just how I was feeling. Shortly after, Joe called me to ask if I was okay.

"Yeah, I'm doing pretty well," I said. I read to Joe what I had written. "This is what I want to read at my mother's funeral."

"That's really nice, Brenda! Are you sure you're okay?"

"Yeah, I'm fine. I am just so glad that I am actually going to be with her. I just want to say, 'Hello, Mom,' and tell her that I love her. That's all I ask." We both started to cry.

He said, "Call me when you get there."

"Okay, I love you."

"I love you too."

I had an eleven o'clock Arizona time flight into Washington, DC. I arrived at five thirty the next morning. Uncle Charles and Aunt Debbie drove three hours to pick me up. Then we had a three-hour drive to the hospital.

I kept saying, "Thank you so much. I just want you to know how much this means to me. How will I ever repay you?" I tried to give them money. They would not take it.

Uncle Charles said, "Brenda, I'm doing this for your mother and father. Your dad is like a brother to me. I would do anything for him. We love your parents. This is not a problem for us. We're glad to get you to her."

We talked the whole way home. The drive seemed like forever. As we were approaching the hospital, I got a text message from Joe. It said, "Ask her to wait for me!"

I thought, *Oh my, Joe is asking for a miracle! There is no way my mom will ever make it two more days.* I did not have the heart to respond to his text message. However, I knew how much they loved each other, and I prayed that, if possible, it would happen.

As we were getting closer to the hospital, my adrenaline started running. My heart started racing. All my words were twisted. All I wanted to say was "Hello, Mom."

My uncle dropped me off right at the front door of the hospital. I went in but didn't know where to go. I could not see or talk but was able to mutter, "Where is she?" People there took me to the elevator. My hands and feet went completely numb. They curled up to the point that I felt paralyzed. As the elevator opened, all I wanted to do was run. However, my hands and feet were not allowing me to.

I thought, *Oh my God, maybe she is dying now. Maybe that is why my hands and feet are numb. She is not dying until I say, "Hello, Mom."*

I had no idea who was with me. I shook my hands and feet as hard as I could and started running down the hallway as fast as I could. I had no idea where I was going. All I knew was I would search and run until I found her! I ran into her room and lay right next to her in her bed.

The first words out of my mouth were "Hello, Mom. I love you, Mom. I'm here, Mom. I'm here, Mom." I still had no idea who was there or what my surroundings were. I was finally with my mother. I knew I would not allow God to take her before I said, "Hello, Mom."

A nurse in the room was taking her vital signs. My mother was awake. She could hardly speak. She had an oxygen mask. As I was lying with her, I saw a packet of rosary beads on her dinner table. I opened and placed them in the shape of a heart on her blanket. I kept saying, "I love you so much, Mom." I told her how sorry I was for not being with her. I just kept talking. My words came out exactly how I wanted them to. However, I could not understand why I could speak so naturally.

I sat next to her for about an hour. My dad and siblings came into the room. We all hugged and kissed each other. As we gathered in her hospital room, my mom started to do what she did best. She tried to comfort our fears by saying everything to take our minds off what was happening.

Shortly after, more family and friends came in. Many people were around her. My dad explained to me what was going on. He said the hospice needed us to make a decision on how to treat her. My mom smirked at me and nodded.

Soon after, the hospice nurse came in while we were all there and explained everything to us. She was so sympathetic to our needs and questions. We sat and cried together. My sister and I fed our mother her dinner. Mom ate a few bites. The nurse came in and told us they were putting her on a ventilator. We did not truly know what to expect. I did not realize my mom would not be able to speak to us. She could not remove this machine as she did the oxygen mask.

David and I stayed with her that night. We did not leave her side. We sat and watched her every breath. Throughout the night, my mom's vital signs kept dropping. David and I were scared to death.

The next morning, as the sun came up, friends and more family came in to see her. I noticed her vitals had started to improve. In the early afternoon, a priest came into the room to pray with us. He gave us another rosary. I placed it on her blanket in the shape of a heart. She had two beautiful hearts on her blanket.

Shortly after, my aunt Louise came into the room with my dad, my sister, and her two kids, Jimmy and Enid. Enid asked me about the rosary beads on the blanket and where they had come from. I told her about the priest who had come in and given them to my mom.

I asked, "Enid, why don't you go find the priest and ask for another one?"

Enid said, "Sure." She got up and walked down the hallway to ask for one more. When Enid came back, she placed the rosary in the shape of a heart on my mom's blanket.

A little while later, I felt extremely overwhelmed. Everybody was there. There was nothing at all we could do for my mom. She had done so much for every one of us. In return, nothing could be done to help her.

I left the room and went downstairs to smoke a cigarette. I sat there for a while, thinking of a way to handle losing her. The thought of my mother not being in my reach and my not having the ability to speak to her—I just could not wrap my head around it. I called Joe and talked to him for a while.

He said, "I will be there as soon as I can. Please tell her to wait for me."

After hanging up with Joe, I walked back into her room. There were so many people in the room who wanted to be with her. They came constantly all day and all night.

Aunt Louise noticed I hadn't taken a shower. "Brenda, you should go home and take a shower. You'll feel much better."

I smiled at her.

She said, "Yeah, go. You stink."

I smiled again. I thought, *Yeah, maybe I'll go home. I will get my mom's car, take a shower, and come back.* I told everyone I was going home to take a shower. Then I thought, *I need to get my mom the most beautiful gown I can find. She needs to look beautiful.*

I went to Boscov's and walked around in circles. Nothing there felt good enough. Very indecisive, I finally found a beautiful dress, some earrings, and a necklace. Still undecided, I took the outfit up to the cashier and muttered, "Does this outfit look okay?"

She said, "Yeah, it's okay."

I felt crushed. I wanted her to say it was beautiful. I wanted her to tell me it was the best outfit she had ever seen. I did not say anything to her. I walked over to the rack, put the gown back, and left, crying.

As I was driving, I realized there would never be a perfect dress for my beautiful mother—at least not on this planet. Nothing was good enough. I drove home to take a quick shower and then went back to the hospital.

Chapter 19

As I walked into Mom's room, Tara was holding a large, pretty flower, as she was looking for a vase to place it in.

I asked, "Where did you get that flower?"

She said, "I picked it out of that flower arrangement out there in the hallway."

I looked at her with a smirk on my face. "Really, Sis? Oh my God, I can't believe you stole that from this Catholic hospital."

"I know, but it's too beautiful to be out there in that hallway in all the construction going on out there! So I took just one for Mommy."

I gave her a look, like, *How wrong are you!*

Not long after, as I walked down the hallway and saw the beautiful arrangement, I thought the same thing: *This is just too beautiful to be out here, in all this construction.* I also picked a flower from the arrangement and placed it in the same vase. Actually, every time I passed the arrangement, I could not help myself. I knew it was wrong, but I justified it because of the construction.

Later on, the time was getting closer to when Joe and my kids would be coming to the hospital. Mom was not well. She was incapable of talking; she was just lying there. The doctors had upped her morphine. My mom was completely unresponsive.

I looked up at the clock. It said two o'clock. I lost it. I felt all these emotions come over me. My heart was racing. My body felt like rubber.

I was crying uncontrollably and repeatedly saying, "I'm so sorry. I'm so sorry." I constantly said the words "I'm so sorry ... I'm so sorry" to David, who was trying to calm me down. I was trying so hard to stop crying, but I could not get myself together. I wanted to be quiet but felt so loud. Therefore, David, Tara, and my friend Lacey walked me downstairs. They talked to me until I felt better.

At two thirty, Joe arrived with Joseph, Gracie, and Kathryn. I felt much better. I kissed them all. We walked up to my mom's room. I walked in and felt something different—something positive. I started to notice what was happening. I noticed the beautiful arrangement Tara and I had built for her. I noticed how many people truly loved my mother. I realized how many lives she had touched. I understood my mom would never have to suffer again.

Joe and the kids were so upset. I did not know how to handle Kathryn. She was only three years old. I thought I could bring her close enough to my mom's room so my mom could hear her voice and know Kathryn was with her. Everyone there made such a fuss over Kathryn. They played with her and asked her about the vacation.

Kathryn often tried to look into the room. She repeatedly said, "Me-Mom. Me-Mom." Therefore, Aunt Louise brought Kathryn closer to the room. With a disgusted look on her face, Kathryn demanded, "Take that off Me-Mom right now!" She had a nasty tone to her voice. She did not take her eyes off her Me-Mom.

Joe was crying hard while holding my mom's hand. He kept putting his head down.

I said to Joe, "It's okay to talk to her. The hospice nurse said she can still hear us."

He started shaking his head and put it down. He continued crying. We all were together.

Mixed emotions were going through my mind. *Maybe she wants us to walk out of the room. Maybe she does not want us to watch her pass on. She really needs to just let go. What is she holding on for? Why does she need to die? I know she will be in a better place. She will no longer suffer, and she will never have another worry. She will be our angel.*

It was getting late. Joe and I took our kids downstairs to get something to eat in the cafeteria. I felt confused as to what my mom would want me to do. I felt guilty for leaving her side. I did not want her to pass away without me with her.

However, the hospice nurse told me, "Don't be surprised if your mother passes while you step out of the room. She may want to go once everyone is out of the room."

I knew my mother would never in a million years want me to watch her go. She knew what that would do to me. She knew every single one of us would be completely devastated. Maybe she wanted me to leave and go home with Joe and the kids. I left and went home.

Shortly after, I got a phone call from David. He asked, "Where are you?"

"Home."

"What?" With a really angry tone to his voice, David asked, "Why did you leave? The nurse just told me that we should take her off the machine. I'm not making that decision on my own."

I yelled back at him. Two minutes later, as I was putting my shoes on, the nurse clicked in on the other line. I clicked over to answer the call. She said, "It would be a good idea to take your mother off the machine. She has been on it for quite some time. Your mother will have bruising around her mouth. She's really dry."

I acknowledged the fact that we could not do this to her anymore. I said, "I'm coming. I will be there in a few minutes." I hung up the phone and drove as fast as I could to the hospital.

I ran up to the lobby where David was standing. He was still upset with me for leaving the hospital. We got into a nasty argument. He said with a nasty tone to his voice, "I can't believe you left me here."

I yelled, "Look, jerk, this is not the time you want to be talking to me with that tone! Believe me, I'm about half-nuts right now. Don't you even think about messing with me."

David walked away. Both of us were so frustrated at the situation we were in. Neither one of us wanted to deal with the fact that our mother was dying.

Our uncle Charles, aunt Debbie, and cousins Jackie and Brianna were all still there with us. I don't believe they ever left our side. My cousins walked with David. Aunt Debbie and Uncle Charles walked with me down the hallway toward my mother's room. As we approached her room, we stood in the hallway as the nurse went in to remove the ventilator from our mother.

The nurse then came out of my mom's room and said, "It's okay. You all can go in now."

Pure adrenaline ran through me. We all walked in. She was lying there, gasping for air. It took me a few minutes to gather myself.

The nurse left and closed the door behind her. David sat at the end of the bed, balling his eyes out, with his hands tightly covering his ears.

I sat next to Mom. I didn't cry. My main goal was to talk my beautiful mother into heaven. I did not feel what I thought I would. I kept talking to her, telling her how beautiful she was, what an amazing mother she had been and always would be to me. I said, "It's going to be the most beautiful place you have ever seen. You are going to be with your mother and Gram. They will be waiting for you. Mom, stop being so stubborn. You will never have to feel pain again. Mom, please just go with Kelly. She needs you up there with her."

As soon as I said those words, she made a small noise, and one teardrop rolled down my mother's face. In that moment, I felt the most amazing, beautiful sensation I have ever felt in my life. This overwhelming love, happiness, and peace came over me. I did not know what to say to those in the room with me. At first, I felt shameful, yet my smile was beaming.

Everyone in the room was so upset and crying. My experience was nothing like theirs. I did not know how to console my little brother. He was extremely upset. I could not imagine my accepting her death so well. What was wrong with me?

We cleaned her room and packed all her belongings. I just could not understand why I felt so beautiful about my mom's death. What I had just witnessed in my mother's hospital room looked horrific. We watched her struggle to gasp for air. I wondered what she had felt, being able to accept the beauty that she was now going to see, feel, and live with in heaven.

We all left. I drove myself. I sat in my car for a few minutes, trying to understand what had just happened and feeling guilty that I was not upset. *How am I going to explain myself to everyone?* I thought. *They will think I do not love her.* I had many thoughts going through my mind, but at the same time, I felt beautiful on the inside. I needed to get my voice out there. I wanted to be heard.

I posted a note on Facebook again. It was really late. I wanted to share my experience with others. I felt extremely connected with God. In addition, I felt powerful; I could not help but wonder why. I went home and lay in my bed.

This was a discovery for me: the true meaning of life. I felt that in every single circumstance in my life, my beautiful mother had been there to guide and teach me along the way. I have always been a reflection of my mother. Through our darkest days, she taught me my truth. It wasn't always what I wanted to hear.

I realized that God had brought her home with him. I felt the beauty in it. My heart was open to accept her death. I did not feel selfish or think, *Why me?* or even think of this as a loss. I believed her moving up and into heaven was a gain for everyone. I thought, *Oh my, thank you, God! Thank you for everything! Thank you for all you have given my beautiful mother and me. Thank you for being the best and most beautiful mother in the whole world.*

The connection of my life is designed for me, not against me. Every single place I have ever been is exactly where I've needed to be. The circumstances and experiences have allowed me to accept layers of truth within.

Although my story comes written in word form, it has also been my driving force. My words, my story, my experiences within—learning how to accept and understand what I was—allowed growth. What exists in you exists within me; we are one. My story has always stayed the same. The only thing that has changed is the way I feel about it. The moment you reach the core person within yourself, you know it. My truth became beautiful the moment I felt the beauty in it!

A Daughter/Mother Kind of Love

I believe God sent me as a gift from above to raise and call your own.
You're a leader, teacher, messenger, and, at times, an enemy.
You're my truest best friend I'll ever see.
You'll throw me a smile to cover the sorrow when you are in the rain,
an action a daughter would know and come to understand.
I'm your mirror you may not always want to see.
You gave when I didn't want or need you,
nor when our words were left unspoken.
It was a gift so large that we couldn't even see.
A little time is all we needed.
Actions needed to be broken.
A hug is what we are.
Perhaps we are each other's angel to rise above and see it all.
You're a strong, amazing woman whom I love and call Mom.
You have your ability to see my life changes.
You have the strength to guide when I fall down.
You had the life lessons you survived long before me.
The rough road willing to grow, we built, lived, and enjoy today.
I am older now, with two daughters of my own.
You molded me into this beautiful woman I now own.
Your footsteps were planted before mine
so I could step in and see my beautiful daughters,

and many to come will hopefully feel this too!
You're designed perfectly for me, the one and only you.
Our bond couldn't go unspoken.
It's just too beautiful and true.
I know you, and I fly high in the sky all because of you.
Much love,
Your daughter

Our Story

Dear Joe,

Thirteen years ago, we became one. Our life together, as I knew, would be perfect. I thought I loved you then! We have unseen problems in each, both love and hate. During our life together, you took me places I never wanted to go. I went anyway. You showed me feelings I never in my lifetime could ever dream of experiencing. I felt them. You showed me the worst in you. I chose to watch. You showed me you could fight back at life. I saw it happen. You did! Your instinct needed help from me when I desperately wanted it and wouldn't ask until I saw you do it. I followed your lead and did the same for myself. You worked so hard to become the man you are, and I feel that you finally love you. I sensed this and wanted to feel that way for myself. You helped me find it. I can feel it. I love me. I showed you there is beauty in this world for you to see. You gave it to me.

Many friends said to me, "I admire what you have together."

They see houses, money, and things, which all never meant anything to me!

Your mother yelled to me, "Do you see how Joseph looks at you?"

I am sorry, but I really did not see it. You told me I was the best person that ever came into your life and you would never, ever leave me. I could not hear you and wanted you to go. My mother understood you when I did not.

A powerful lady in our life said, "I know you don't want to see this. You and Joseph have the best marriage on the block."

I thought, *Hell no! I will never, ever feel that.*

Because of you, I know I love you more than ever. I hear it in your voice. I see it in your eyes. I feel it in your touch. I want you. I need you. I got you.

From my heart to yours, you are the best person that ever walked into my life. How I feel today, I would not want to change one piece of our life together. I never expected any of this. You give it anyway! Thank you for all your gifts.

Love always,
Brenda

~Big Hug~

Dear Dad,

It is so hard for me to sit back and watch you sit in pain. I feel sad because I know I am able to take pain out of you. However, I feel you do not believe I can. These last couple of days, I have been wondering if I should even try. I feel useless if I do not and sad because you will need to feel the pain of your life. I completely understand your past. I want to give you the chance to see yourself in a new way for what you are meant to be, only for yourself and not for me. I wonder if you will ever get the chance to see a new life. Will you ever be able to see that man in the mirror and be the proud man that you should have always been—to feel like you, like yourself, for what and who you are? I believe you deserve to be set free. I feel you lived in pain most of your life and were never able to understand. There really is better for you, Dad. You just need to believe you deserve it.

I know I said some mean words to you when I was young. I didn't mean them. I said it because I was angry at you, just the same as you hurt me. Words can be very powerful! Back then, I never got the chance to really get to know you because I didn't allow myself the chance. I really want to show you now. I'm able to forgive myself for my past. I believe this is our time in our lives that we are meant to have. We are to share our stories with each other. So many years have passed us by, wasted. We can do much better than our past. I know it! You will need to forgive me for my past, my words, my thoughts, and my actions toward you. I have no wall anymore. I'm able to understand feelings with an open mind now. (I got help when I needed it most.)

You lost the love of your life to cancer. She always saw something special about you, but because of your own childhood pain and Vietnam, you thought no one could ever understand what you saw and felt there and still carry with you. But she could! She loved you unconditionally. You always gave her some kind of secure feeling. I'm not sure if you know this, but you were her rock. She told me so. I believe the same holds true for you.

Now that your rock is not here, you're lost and broken. Dad, it's really okay. I need you to know I've reached the feeling of brokenness. Our reasons are different. But I have been there. I know what that feels like. Also I know that's the best place for us to get our feelings out and reach what is better for ourselves.

I just wanted you to know that I really do love you and it kills me to see you living in this much pain. Mommy would want you to feel better about yourself. I know she would! She loved you very much and only wanted the best for you. Now is your chance to find it.

Love,
Brenda

Dear Samantha,

You may not realize how many lives you have touched, along with the drive and passion you have inside to teach others. I need you to know exactly what you gave me.

As I looked inside, not liking what I saw and placing blame on all around me, I came into your office with mixed emotions. I was not able to understand. I was feeling right, perfect, stupid—loss, shame, and anger. I was a no-good bastard, a piece of shit. I felt hate, weakness—alone, fragile, and broken. I felt, acted, and owned each and every negative feeling for myself. These self-destructive feelings almost destroyed me.

I now own my story. It's a part of me. I share with others so they can see. I lost the shame. Need has taken over. My true passion is to teach right from my heart. I understand it's only a cycle lived. I felt and understood. We can all choose to rise above.

Negative feelings were a part of me, but I am no longer attached. My life will never be perfect. You gave me the tools to see me through. You walked into my life for a perfect reason. You lifted me up when I needed to speak the words of my battle. You sat there to listen with your knowledge and sweet heart. You had understanding for me to see a brighter start. You were spreading your love without even knowing. I reached high above. All I can see is how beautiful this life is.

Oh, boy, I'm free! My "thank you" will never compare to this beautiful life you have given me. You're the most powerful gift that heaven has ever sent me!

You will always and forever be in my heart.

Much love,
Brenda

Printed in the United States
By Bookmasters